Wind on the River

by Laurie Lawlor

JAMESTOWN PUBLISHERS

a division of NTC/CONTEMPORARY PUBLISHING GROUP
Lincolnwood, Illinois USA

For my great-grandfather
Samuel Wallace Mills (1847–1922)
who joined Company E, 43rd Regiment
Wisconsin Volunteers of the Union Army
when he was 17

Cover Credits
    Design: Herman Adler Design Group
    Illustration: David Schweitzer
    Timeline
        Left: ©1992 North Wind Pictures
        Right: ©1998 North Wind Pictures

Page iv: Library of Congress; page 152: U.S. National Archives;
page 153: Courtesy of Maryland Park Foundation;
page 154: Alabama Department of Archives and History,
Montgomery, Alabama; page 156: Montana Historical Society, Helena

ISBN: 0-8092-0582-3 (hardbound)
ISBN: 0-8092-0624-2 (softbound)

Published by Jamestown Publishers,
a division of NTC/Contemporary Publishing Group, Inc.,
4255 West Touhy Avenue,
Lincolnwood (Chicago), Illinois 60712-1975 U.S.A.
©2000 Laurie Lawlor
Manufactured in the United States of America.

99 00 01 02 03 04 05 06 07 08 09 ML 0 9 8 7 6 5 4 3 2 1

Montana and Dakota Territories During the Civil War

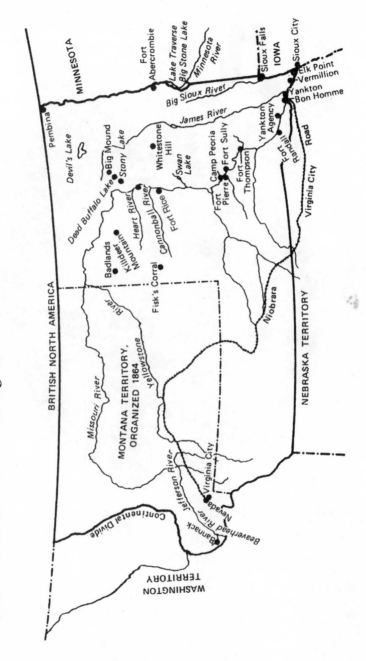

Private Edwin Francis Jemison, 2nd Louisiana Regiment,
Confederate States of America

Chapter 1

Griff awkwardly leaned his gun against a tree and stood in the darkness outside the circle of firelight. He was waiting for the right moment. The other men didn't notice him. They were too busy drinking Oh Be Joyful and bragging about the magnificent victory at Chancellorsville. No one could whip General Lee. No one. The smoky bonfire made from Yankee fence rails sputtered and snapped. The South Carolina boys had invaded Pennsylvania and were camped on Union soil for the first time. They felt fine. Just fine. And anything seemed possible this mild drizzling evening on the last day of June 1863. Anything at all.

Mosquitoes whined in Griff's ears. He did not wave away the biting insects. He needed both hands to hold tight to the heavy, cumbersome bundle hidden under his coat. "Hey," he said and took a step forward, "you all hungry?"

"Come on out of that coat, Griff. I see your head. I know you're in there," said Stevens, who was always quick with a joke.

"What you got for us this time?" Wiley demanded. He licked his thick lips.

Griff glanced over his shoulder. He moved his arms, and something thudded on the ground between his dirty, bare feet. A fine fat pig glimmered motionless in the firelight.

For a moment, no one spoke. No one moved.

"You done did it this time," Wiley said in a reverent tone. "Ham dinner. Thank the Lord."

Stevens stood up and slapped Griff on his skinny shoulder so hard he nearly toppled. "You've got the lightest fingers in the Confederate Army."

"I know," Griff replied with a trace of pride.

Powers took his knife from his belt and wiped the blade on his greasy pants leg. "You wasn't seen, was you?"

"Only the captain spied me," Griff said.

The men groaned. "We're doomed," whispered Stevens.

"What happened when he stopped you?" Powers demanded.

"He asks, 'What you got there?' " Griff paused dramatically to make sure everyone was listening.

"So what'd you tell him?" Powers said.

" 'Pig,' I says. So he tells me, 'Are you aware of rules against such practices as shooting hogs?' And I say, 'Yes,

2

sir. I know it's against the rules, but I killed this pig in self defense.' "

"How's that?" said Wiley, who was nearly 18 but none too bright.

"Shut up and let him tell it," Stevens demanded.

"I says to the captain, 'Well, I was coming up to camp, and I hears some fierce roaring. First I thinks it might be a haunt—maybe some kind of wailing Yankee ghost. When I turns and looks, I see a pig come out of a hole in the ground, fixing to attack,' " Griff continued. " 'So just before it got to me, I fired and the pig was killed.' "

The men chuckled. "How'd you keep the captain from appropriating our dinner?" Stevens asked.

"Gave him a fine silver Yankee watch," Griff said. "Better get to butchering this pig 'fore he finds out that watch is broke."

Powers and Stevens quickly skinned and butchered the pig. When the sweet-smelling meat began to roast over the fire, Wiley turned to Griff and said in admiration, "I swear you could steal the buttons off the coat of a wide-awake old man."

"True enough." Griff shoved his hands deep in his pockets and pulled out the linen handkerchief requested by Stevens, the pipe that Powers wanted, and the bunch of green apples for Wiley. "Now pay up, fellows. Don't forget: five cents Federal equals two dollars Confederate."

Each man gave Griff what he'd promised—plugs of tobacco, which were good for trade, Yankee greenbacks or

Confederate currency. "Pretty soon Confederate money won't be worth the paper it's printed on," Stevens said and shook his head.

"One thing's for certain. Griff, you'll be a rich man before this war's over," Powers grumbled as he handed over his money.

"I surely will," Griff replied. But when no one was looking, he gave Wiley something small and cold and shiny.

"What's this?" Wiley asked, examining the object in his bearlike hand.

"Put it to your ear and give it a shake," Griff said.

Wiley did as he was told. The little silver bell made a pretty sound. Wiley grinned. He rang it again. Suddenly, the big man's smile vanished. "What do I pay?"

"Nothing."

"Nothing?"

"It's a gift," said Griff, who knew that he hadn't given anything away. He had only made a wise investment in the biggest, strongest man in the company.

Wiley shut his baby-blue eyes and rang the bell. With a gentle smile, he tucked Griff's present inside his pocket.

After finishing every last bit of their delicious dinner, the men lounged around the fire. Stevens picked his teeth with a whittled piece of twig. Powers smoked his pipe. As the fire burned low, some spoke longingly of home and wives and little children left behind. Others murmured the names of sweethearts whose beauty they swore they would never forget.

"These Yankee girls is so ugly that a man hates to look," Powers declared. "I thought it well to avoid their glances to keep from hurting my eyes. This is the truth, certain."

The other men hooted.

Then no one said a word. In the silence, it seemed as if every man were contemplating something secret and inexpressible.

"My little boy's why I joined up," Stevens said finally. "I want him to think of his father as a hero. Somebody who did his duty for God and country."

"To glorious Dixie!" Powers said and raised his tin cup.

Stevens raised his cup. "To glorious South Carolina!"

Then they drank again to Dixie and South Carolina and General Lee.

"You're awful quiet, Griff," Powers said. He belched and swiveled a bug-eyed gaze in Griff's direction. "You're fighting for the cause of your country, ain't you?"

Griff shrugged and poked the dying fire with a stick.

Powers squinted, which only made him look meaner. "Well sure enough you must miss something about the Carolina up-country."

"Don't miss nothing," Griff said quietly.

"Strange thing to hear tell from a boy of 15 so far away from home first time in his life." Powers grinned as if he were enjoying Griff's obvious discomfort. "Maybe you're just trying to fool us about not missing your pa and ma."

Griff did not answer. He simply stood up and walked away from the fire.

The next day at first light, someone shouted, "Fall in!"

Griff sat up, still aching from a bad sleep on hard ground. He slipped on his dilapidated shoes, rolled his blanket, slung his knapsack over his shoulder and his canteen around his neck. The men stepped quickly into a fast pace down the Pennsylvania pike. Like sleepwalkers, they did not seem to notice when they nearly stumbled on each other's heels. There were thousands of soldiers—a rolling gray sea of ragged legs and gleaming muskets.

"Strong taint of battle," Powers said. He expertly sniffed the cloudy, close morning that smelled of unwashed bodies and dust and sweat.

Nobody spoke. They were all under light marching orders, which meant they had to move swiftly and with only the most necessary items carried along. Before they left, Griff had seen Stevens tuck photographs of his wife and child inside his pocket. Powers hid an envelope with letters from his mother inside his shirt, and Wiley carried a little prayer book with a lock of hair pressed between the pages inside his knapsack.

Griff had taken along his money and tobacco, tied tight inside a grimy handkerchief. As if in a dream, he felt inside his pocket to make sure his little bundle was still there. He tried not to think that this time he might die. Nobody ever said such things aloud. But the others must have felt it too, Griff was certain.

In the distance came the sullen boom of artillery, and then the long, uninterrupted crackling of muskets and rifles. The noise reminded Griff of the snapping and popping of a pile of dried-up brush when first set to burning. He and the others had been in enough battles to sense that something big—very big—was about to happen. Somebody said this unit and all the rest were headed for some place called Gettysburg.

As on all marches, the men hurried up, then waited, then hurried up some more. There was no sense an ordinary soldier ever had as to the meaning of the marching forward and the halting. Griff never knew for sure what was going to happen till the real fighting started. He looked around at the countryside to keep his mind occupied. They passed through rich, green farmland filled with fat, grazing cattle and orchards heavy with fruit. Bees buzzed in orderly hives. Silver-green corn stood strong and tall. Pennsylvania farms did not look anything like the worn-out old fields Griff had left behind.

Without warning, the men were told to stop and sit and wait for an hour. The uncertainty was unbearable. Up ahead, Griff could hear the slam of artillery that sounded like a summer thunderstorm growing stronger, closer. *Boom! Boom! Boom!* Then the sound changed. When he closed his eyes, he thought he was hearing a large canebrake on fire.

"Fall in!"

He kept marching. He and the other men turned off the main pike on to a dusty country road. And suddenly they were wading through a wheat field. The waist-high, golden-ripe wheat bent and waved in the wind. *Hissssss!* Like a warning. The men stood there among the trampled, but otherwise perfect stalks. Griff brushed a fly from his face. He drank the last swig of water from his canteen. *Someone should harvest before the rain comes.* He imagined a red-faced Yankee boy his age with his shirt off, carrying a scythe.

The soldiers moved forward and flattened more grain. They had been ordered not to fire, not to speak, not to holler. Just march. Sweat poured off Griff. He looked to his left and saw Powers grinning hungrily as if he wanted to kill somebody. Stevens's nervous eyes darted back and forth to distant trees. Wiley mumbled something that sounded like a bewildered prayer.

Always at this moment before a battle began, Griff felt as if he were about to step off a cliff. His heart seemed to stop beating. He could barely breathe. He was on the edge of something, he knew it, and his nerves jangled uncontrollably. Fear pricked up in his mind like mice in a bag of pumpkin seeds. He wished he'd thought to wear his shirt inside-out for good luck. Too late now.

Nervous silence shrouded the other men too. Some gazed off into space. Some gnawed on their lips. Some drummed their fingers absentmindedly against their gun stocks. Standing, waiting. Standing, waiting. And all the while, invisible deadly guns cracked and rumbled ahead.

"Dang. Sharp skirmishing in front," Stevens said in an exaggerated nasal twang.

Somehow his ridiculous words called them all back to life. Powers guffawed. Wiley began to chuckle too. Even Griff couldn't help himself. It was such a relief to laugh.

They marched forward again. The wheat whispered. They stopped. A man in another regiment broke rank and ran to hide behind a tree at the edge of the field. Clearly, his nerves were gone. Griff watched. They all watched. *He could be me,* Griff thought and felt ashamed.

"Get that man back in line!" a captain screamed.

Someone tried. But the man wouldn't budge. He clung to the tree as if to his very life.

Suddenly, the general rushed up astride a strong prancing horse, which made him seem even more enormous and powerful. "I'll move him!" the general cried loud enough for everyone to hear. He whipped out his gleaming saber and dealt the man a blow.

The man fell. He did not get up. Nobody knew who the soldier was. Nobody asked. They all looked away as if they hadn't seen. Everyone, that is, except Griff.

He cringed. His ears rang. And once again he heard a low, familiar voice, drunken and dangerous, calling his name. He shivered and opened and shut his sweating hands. How many desperate hours had he hid inside that chicken coop—his palms and knees embedded with sharp slivers and chicken manure—waiting for the terrible voice to go away? . . .

Someone shoved Griff, jolting him from his thoughts. "Get moving!"

9

Griff gave one last look at the place where the soldier had fallen under the blade of his own general. Griff stumbled forward. Joining up had been his escape. How was he to know that officers could be just as cruel as Pa, with his endless, pointless beatings back in Carolina? How was he to know that these blind, terrified soldiers would remind him of Ma, who always managed to look the other way and pretend not to see?

For the first time, Griff considered deserting. The thought twisted deep inside his gut like a writhing copperhead caught in the teeth of a haymow.

"Advance!"

From the division ahead came the ghostly shriek, the Rebel yell. "Who-who-ey! WHO-WHO-EY!"

Artillery fire crashed. Shells hurtled and exploded. Minie balls sizzed through the air and bounded harmlessly into the wheat or thudded savagely into bodies. Men screamed in pain. Horses whinnied piteously. Stevens fell first. Then Powers twisted, headless, and plunged. Griff ducked. He dodged to the left and to the right like a mouse in a trap desperate to escape. The bullets came so fast from the left and the right, he did not even think to load and fire his own gun. *We're all going to die. All of us,* he thought.

Bodies piled up quickly. Griff tripped. He plunged into the armless embrace of a corpse, staggered to his feet again, and kept running through the smoke and explosions.

"Where do you think you're going?" a bleeding officer on a horse shouted at him. He waved his revolver. "Die like a man, not like a dog! Get in line!"

Griff heard Pa's voice. He felt Pa's hot, sour whiskey-breath on the back of his neck, and he ran faster. He dropped his precious knapsack. He threw his blanket behind him and leapt over crumpled, bleeding bodies. Some dead. Some nearly dead. Moaning and crying out for help.

But he did not stop. His legs seemed to have a life of their own now. They carried him to safety in a small, quiet woods beyond a stone wall. He did not know where he was. He had run so fast, so hard, so long. Maybe he wasn't even in Pennsylvania anymore. He threw himself down in the shattered, bloody ferns and covered himself with branches. Curled in a ball, he shook uncontrollably. He pressed his cheek to the earth and felt the ground rumble and quake. *War's not the thing it's bragged up to be. I got to see the elephant, and to tell the truth, I don't care about seeing him very much no more.*

His hands and forehead were bleeding. His coat was torn. His gun was gone. He shut his eyes tight and felt himself falling into a deep sleep, as dark and impenetrable as the inside of a bottomless well.

Hours later, sundown came. The heavy firing stopped. When Griff finally awoke, he knew he was in trouble. Someone was bent over him, rifling through his clothes.

When Griff began to protest in a loud groggy voice, a

pair of hands pushed him away impatiently. "This one's still alive," the voice said in disgust. The shadowy figure moved on to the next slumped body. Other scavengers, outlined in the darkness, moved swiftly, removing rings and buttons, eyeglasses, and watches. They worked silently.

Griff sat up, trembling. His mouth filled with a sour taste. He felt overwhelmed by nausea. In the past, he had always been the one to do the scavenging. This time, he was the one left for dead. He shoved his hands into his empty pockets. *My money!* Angrily, he pounded the ground with his fist. Every bit of his earnings was gone. *Now what?*

All around him came the sound of a thousand pitiful voices calling for water. "Help me! Help me!" they cried.

"Someone put me out of my misery!"

Griff put his hands over his ears. What should he do now? He had to think. What had happened to the rest of his unit? Where could he find them? He crouched, stood, and felt dizzy with hunger. He had not eaten all day. Slowly, he bent over and moved his hands among the ferns to locate his knapsack. Then he remembered that he had tossed it into the field while he was running. All he was able to find was his empty canteen. He put it around his neck.

"This is my territory. Ain't none of yours," a scavenger hissed.

Griff took a few steps backward, nearly falling over a

dead, bloated horse. So many corpses lay heaped on the ground that he felt as if he were walking in a crowded hog pen—only all the animals had died. He had to get away from this place. He rubbed his blood-stiff hair and began walking. The night was hot, and the smell of smoke and death was overpowering. In the distance he saw flickering light. Campfires. The familiar glow made him move faster. On and on he staggered. The light grew brighter.

"Who goes there?" a picket shouted. In the darkness came the unmistakable sound of a gun being loaded.

"John Griffin Allen, sir," Griff said nervously. In his mind he rehearsed his excuse: *Wasn't deserting, sir. Got separated from my fellows.*

"Regiment?" the hard voice demanded.

"South Carolina Volunteers."

The picket laughed.

That was when Griff knew he'd made a terrible mistake. The biggest mistake of his life.

Chapter 2

For the next eight long months, Griff was held as a prisoner of war with 11,000 other Confederates at Point Lookout, a Yankee hellhole on a desolate flat point of land at the junction of the Potomac River and the Chesapeake Bay in Maryland. Griff and the other underfed, shivering prisoners were crammed into the camp's 20 acres, which were bare of trees or vegetation of any kind.

In summer, the camp was scorched by sun. In winter, cold winds whipped across the sand and battered the flimsy white tents that housed the prisoners. Eventually, the effect of glaring white canvas, bright sand, and the constant reflection of the surrounding water caused some men to develop a peculiar form of night blindness. Crowded, dirty conditions helped quickly spread measles, smallpox, and dysentery.

Griff and the others knew that if they got sick, the worst place to end up was the camp's hospital. Most who went in never came out. As soon as a patient died, the body was taken to the Dead House. No one bothered to change the hospital bed sheets before another patient's arrival. Once a day a two-horse wagon came to haul bodies, like cordwood, from the Dead House to the prison cemetery. Here they were buried in mass graves; long trenches seven feet wide and three feet deep. By the end of February 1864, the prison cemetery contained more than a thousand Rebels. The only reminder that they had ever inhabited Point Lookout were plain wooden boards hastily marked with their names.

Griff, however, had no intention of joining the peaceful ranks of the deceased. On this particular cold, blustery morning in March 1864, Griff and the 11 other prisoners who shared his tent coughed and crawled out into the open for roll call.

"Line up!" shouted a brutish guard named Beadle.

The same as every morning, the prisoners were searched for weapons while their tent was combed for smuggled guns—or, better still—delicacies mailed from home.

"Who's this contraband belong to?" Beadle demanded. He held up a small bit of sugar cake wrapped in a dirty rag.

No one spoke. Griff could not believe how stupid one of his tent mates must have been to leave something so valuable so badly hidden.

"I'm taking this for inspection," Beadle said, pocketing the cake.

Griff shot a quick glance at the "fresh fish," three new prisoners from Georgia and Tennessee, who had arrived the week before. Already, they seemed to have lost interest in everything. Hour after hour, day after day, they sat in the tent and gazed dully into space. They wouldn't last the month.

With inspection over, Griff grabbed his tin cup and elbowed his way through the crowd to the nearest pump—one of only a handful in the camp. Already, 40 men were lined up for a chance to sip the brackish, foul-tasting water. In less than an hour, breakfast rations consisting of coffee and small loaves of stale bread would be distributed. The next meal of the day would be dinner: half a pint of thin bean or carrot soup sprinkled with vinegar to prevent scurvy, and a two-ounce scrap of grizzled meat. Griff knew he didn't have much time.

"You in?" he whispered to Wallace, one of his best customers.

"Are you addressing me?" Wallace said and sniffed. Once a young dandy from a tidewater plantation, who had joined the Virginia Cavalry in a broad-rimmed hat with a swooping feather, he was now as lousy, ragged, and dirty as the rest of them. Even so, Wallace had no trouble bribing Beadle and the other guards with money that had mysteriously arrived from his family. "It is galling for a gentleman to be absolutely and entirely subject to the demands of men who, in private life, are my inferiors."

Griff clenched his fist, but thought better of the idea. *Why ruin everything?* For months, the other prisoners had enjoyed the popular weekly louse fights that Griff had staged on the side of his canteen, the ring marked with a charcoal circle. Two hungry lice were ceremoniously selected from the billions inhabiting the camp. The lice were placed back-to-back in the center of the circle. Everyone cheered and watched to see which would survive the fight to the finish. Before every match, wages were placed. Somehow Griff always managed to take a comfortable percentage of the winnings. He had a thriving business going as long as the bribed guards left him alone.

Carefully, he glanced up at the top of the 14-foot-tall wooden fence that surrounded the prison pen. Looking down at him in amusement from the catwalk was one of the many Negro Union guards. The soldier spat and smiled, revealing brilliant white teeth.

"Bottom rail has got on top," grumbled Wallace, looking up at the grinning soldier. "Was there ever such a thing in civilized warfare?"

"Stupid darky," Griff replied. Somehow he felt better saying the word and secretly pointing his dog finger on his right hand to bring the guard bad luck. He turned to Wallace again. "Right smart number of bets placed already. What's your wager?"

"One pocketknife, two hardtack crackers, and five chews of tobacco."

Griff whistled under his breath, impressed by Wallace's reckless bet. He solemnly shook hands with Wallace to seal the deal.

On his way to collect his breakfast rations, Griff glanced out beyond the gate toward the roiling gray Potomac River. Something caught his eye. A barrel bobbed in the waves. Some afternoons, even in cold weather, prisoners who had displayed good behavior were allowed to bathe in the river at high tide.

Wouldn't take much to slip my head under that barrel and drift up river. Keep near to the shore then take to the woods, Griff thought. He sighed, watching the rotten wooden barrel float out of sight. Deep down, he knew that an escape from Point Lookout was nearly impossible. Every minute, they were watched by guards on the fence. Anyone who crossed the "deadline," a ditch inside the stockade fence, would be shot. Artillery and infantry regiments were stationed on the opposite shore to catch runaways. Gunboats patrolled the waters surrounding the camp. Escapees who were caught were gunned down or, worse yet, tortured. Guards like Beadle seemed to take pleasure in stringing up runaways by their thumbs, with the tips of their toes barely touching the ground.

"Hey, Griff!" someone shouted.

Griff crouched on the ground and cradled against his chest what was left of his bread. A tall man, gaunt and bent, stumbled toward him. Was he going to fight? Or did he have something to offer in trade? Maybe a recently caught rat that Griff could cook and eat. "What you want?"

The man looked down at Griff with sad, hollowed eyes. "Don't remember me?"

Griff shook his head. "How'd you know my name?" He slipped his hand near his ankle, where he kept a small hidden knife blade tied. There were plenty of crazy men in camp. Crazy hungry. Crazy homesick. And just plain crazy.

The man thrust a finger inside his shirt. Griff jumped to his feet as quick as a cat and edged backward. The man did not lunge at him. Instead he kept smiling. He pointed to something that hung from a grimy string around his neck. It made a soft, sweet ringing noise.

Griff tried to think. Where had he heard that bell? Where had he seen those eyes? "Wiley?" he whispered in disbelief. "That you?" The faint twinge of happiness surprised him. It was such an unfamiliar emotion. "Been so long since I seen anybody familiar. What happened to you? What happened to the others?"

"Most all went up the spout. Dead at Gettysburg," Wiley said. His smile vanished. The way he brought his finger to his lower lip reminded Griff of a fretful child suddenly forced to remember what he had been trying so hard to forget. "I have went through a heap of narrow escapes since I last seen you, Griff. Got shot through the leg and arm, and laid in that field nearly two days. Nobody to help me. Nobody noticed."

Griff squirmed, recalling how many fallen soldiers he had leapt over while trying to escape.

"Was your bell what saved me," Wiley continued. "When my voice done finished and I didn't have no energy left to call out, I rang that bell over and over, and somebody came. Somebody took care of me. Got me to a hospital and fixed me up good. Only problem was, they was Yankees. And when I got better they puts me in prison, but that's all right 'cause I seen Jesus. I know now that the Confederacy is founded on sin."

Griff thrust his hand over Wiley's mouth. He looked around nervously. "You shut up," he whispered. "People been stabbed for words like that. Want to get us both killed?"

Wiley struggled free. His baby-blue eyes were shining now. "I'm going to take the oath."

"What oath?" Griff wondered if Wiley were bumfuzzled or just plain deranged.

"Oath of allegiance," Wiley explained eagerly. "Join up with the Yankees. Go north. Only way out of this place. Some of the Union boys told me that when they brought me here yesterday."

"Join the Yankees?" Griff asked. He eyed Wiley suspiciously. What if Wiley was a spy? "I don't understand."

Wiley looked around and hunched over, as if he were relating a very important secret. "Tomorrow the Union man with a red sash 'cross his chest brings his big blank book. Going to ask the prisoners questions and have them sign their names in private. Then they turn into Yankees and go free from prison forever."

"What kind of questions?"

Wiley rubbed his big hands together. "Four questions. That's all I know. Say 'yes-yes-yes,' but when they comes to the last one, 'Do you wish to go south?' you say, 'No, sir.' That's what they told me. I'm ready. Thank the Lord. I'm going to be free. Hallelujah!"

Griff pondered Wiley's strange ideas. He wondered if he were telling the truth or just imagining an impossible freedom.

Sure enough, later that day Griff heard the rumor from Wallace, who had heard it from a guard, that there would be special Union visitors coming the very next day. Griff made up his mind, but he kept his thoughts and his plans to himself the way he always did. He'd take the oath, if one were offered. What did he care about Confederate ideals? Words. Stupid words. He'd do anything, be anyone. He'd go north, or anywhere else the Yankees sent him—as long as he escaped from this prison. *Besides, I know I'll never go home again. Never.*

Evening came and the whole camp buzzed with news about the oath of allegiance. Naturally, fights broke out between those who would rather remain in prison and die for the glorious Confederacy and those who were willing to switch sides. Wiley, when cornered by two thugs from Mississippi, simply shielded his face with his big hands, palms outward. Griff watched the beating with the other spectators. He neither called for wagers nor lifted a finger to help a fellow soldier from South Carolina.

Chapter 3

During the next several weeks, more than 8,000 prisoners were interviewed. Some "swallowed the pill," as they called taking the oath. Others refused. Griff was glad when he was finally told that he had officially become a private in the newly formed First U.S. Volunteer Infantry—his ticket to freedom. Griff, Wiley, Wallace and nearly a thousand other "transfugees," as they were named, left Point Lookout in late April 1864 and boarded the convoy ship *George Henry* bound for Norfolk, Virginia.

After their arrival in Virginia, they were given new Yankee uniforms. For the first time, Griff owned factory-made shoes with soles that didn't flap open. He had a brand-new knapsack and a fine coat and trousers. When he studied himself in the looking glass, he noticed that he still had the same dark, impenetrable eyes, heavy brows, big ears, and small mouth. There wasn't any more peach fuzz gracing his upper lip than the last time he checked. Yet somehow in his new clothing, he had hoped to be transformed. He adjusted his cap visor so that it looked just like a Yankee's, and he sighed with disappointment.

On July 27, the First U.S. Volunteers were given guns and marched down to Elizabeth City, North Carolina, where they stole a few horses and some bales of cotton, shot at some fleeing snipers, and then marched back to Norfolk. It was a foolish, cowardly attack—not a real battle like Gettysburg or the other engagements that Griff relived almost every night in his nightmares. He suspected that the entire exercise was designed to give their pompous Yankee officers, dressed up in golden braids and shining brass buttons, something to do.

One hot afternoon in early August, Griff, Wallace, and Wiley relaxed in the shade after another endless drill at the Norfolk camp. Griff leaned back against a tree. Life did not seem so bad as a Yankee. The food was plentiful. He had his own wool blanket that he did not have to share with anyone. No one could tell he was really a Southerner until he opened his mouth.

Suddenly, pale Colonel Dimon galloped past on his horse. A young, vain 23-year-old from Boston, he was serious, strait-laced, and notoriously pious. His hair was dark, his eyes pale gray. He bobbed unmercifully up and down in the saddle in a way that would have put a Confederate cavalryman to shame.

"Ever notice," Griff drawled when the colonel was out

24

of sight, "how these Yankee big brass ain't worth a bunch of low country cow ticks when it comes to riding?"

"If I was you, I wouldn't let on so loud," Wiley said and yawned. He lay on his back, covered his face with his hat and took a nap. Since he'd left prison, Wiley had slowly put on weight. Every day he looked stronger and appeared more like his old self.

Wallace, who was busy writing yet another letter to yet another girl he had met in Norfolk, looked up and said, "Have you ever considered what might happen to us if Confederates take us captive and find out what we did?"

"You mean how we turned into Yankees?" Griff said.

Wallace nodded. "If the Rebs don't kill and mutilate us first, they'll send us for sure to Andersonville Prison. I've heard that's ten times worse than Point Lookout."

Griff took a deep breath. Sometimes when it was dark and he was on patrol, he spied lingering shapes with cruel eyes darting among the trees. Maybe they were haunts. Were they watching him? Did they know who he really was? "You're just trying to rile me," Griff said. He tried to laugh as if he didn't care.

Solemnly, Wallace shook his head. "I'm telling the truth. My family disinherited me for taking the oath. They wrote and told me I disgraced our good name and the cause of the Confederacy. I can never go home. We're called Galvanized Yankees now, and Confederates hate us worse than death."

Griff did not say anything for several moments. He never considered that by taking the oath he had put himself in any danger. Nothing could have been worse than wretched Point Lookout. As a brand-new Yankee, he'd just have to keep his eye out for trouble. He knew how to take care of himself.

One afternoon in mid-August, the First Volunteers were unexpectedly ordered to move out on the transport ship called *Continental*. "We're bound for the western frontier to fight Indians," announced Wallace, who always seemed to know what would happen before it did. Griff and the others quickly packed up their few possessions.

"I ain't never been any farther west than Mississippi," Wiley confided.

"Don't worry," Griff replied with a perfectly straight face. "I know a cure if you feel homesickness coming on. Just sew a good charge of gunpowder on the inside of your shirt near the neck."

"That work?" Wiley asked suspiciously.

"If it don't, it'll blow your head straight off," Griff said, grinning. Somehow, leaving Southern soil brought Griff a kind of relief. He felt as if he were finally escaping the dark shadows of a place where there seemed to be nothing but sorrows and troubles.

On the August morning that he and the others marched aboard the *Continental*, the sun shone and the blue sky was brilliant and clear. For the first time in ever so long, Griff sensed a vague kind of hope—something strange and unfamiliar. Maybe everything would work out fine after all.

"Hallelujah!" Wiley declared and held up his hands

like a preacher man. As he pranced, the bell around his neck jangled. "I believe Providence is on our side. We have not got nothing to fear but will prove to the world that we are right this time."

"Praise the Lord!" another soldier murmured.

"I confess it's a relief to finally know who the enemy is," Wallace said. He stood on the deck with the others. He filled his pipe with fresh tobacco and lit it. "Indians are barbarians—worse than darkies. Indians are not really even humans. We, on the other hand, are the superior civilizers. What could be simpler? If the Indians resist our enlightened Christian ideas, we must kill them. It's very efficient, really."

"I hear they're pretty good fighters," Griff said.

"Pah!" Wallace replied. He took a fresh draft from his pipe and blew a ring of smoke. "We have repeating rifles and modern artillery. And what do they have? Crude bows and arrows. Maybe some spears. Our western frontier war will be child's play. Over in just a few months."

Griff sat on the deck and leaned against the cabin wall in the warm comfort of the sunlight. The steamship rode the rolling waves with a soothing rocking motion. He did not feel the least bit seasick. *Perhaps I'll become a sailor*, he thought. A swift nudge woke him from his reverie.

"You seen her?" Wiley whispered.

"Who?" Griff replied irritably.

"The lady," Wiley said. "Real Virginia lady on board!" He spoke with so much excitement that spit flew from his mouth.

Griff jumped to his feet and surveyed the crowded deck. Southern belles were such an unusual sight that they were studied with great deliberation by all soldiers. Beyond a knot of eager men with their hats off, a fancy first-class woman delicately held on to her bright green bonnet so that it would not fly away in the wind. Her skin was pale. She wore a sweeping long, black skirt with a strange kind of contraption in the back that made her look oddly puffy. The wind billowed her full skirt so hard that Griff and the others had a glimpse of her high-buttoned shoes. He felt amazed by the mysterious sight. He had never suspected that such women even had feet.

"Name's Mrs. Elizabeth Cardwell. Married to Private Patrick Cardwell from Virginia," Wiley whispered in Griff's ear. "Ain't she got pretty eyes a-peeping out from under that bonnet? She's going West with us. I never seen the boys in finer spirits."

Suspiciously, Griff watched the giggling Mrs. Cardwell as she plucked the sleeve of her husband, who seemed to be trying to shield her from the wind. When her handkerchief blew from her hand and tumbled across the deck, Private Cardwell leapt after it and brought it back with a formal bow.

"Lowps just like some fool rabbit," Griff murmured, convinced that the couple were still courting. "Don't act like no married people I ever saw. Seem more like they're sparking."

"She's married for sure," Wiley said with indignation. "That's the only reason Colonel let her come. Don't you go smirching her honor."

Griff rolled his eyes.

He did not pay much attention to the mystifying Mrs. Cardwell again until the regiment landed in New York City. On August 17, the First Volunteers marched through the hot, crowded streets to the railroad station, where they would board a train for Chicago. All seemed disorder and confusion. There were plenty of whiskey peddlers and vendors selling fruit and every kind of food imaginable. Griff wondered what kind of money he could make in such a fabulous, wide-awake place—the biggest, dirtiest city he had ever visited in his life. To his utter astonishment, he saw Wallace spend nearly all of his available cash on a big bouquet of flowers.

"What do you need those for?" Griff demanded as he pushed his way through the crowd.

Wallace did not reply. He held the bright flowers in one hand, put his other behind his back and made a deep bow before Mrs. Cardwell. She seemed thrilled to receive such a gift, even though the weather was so stifling that the flowers immediately began to wilt.

Griff decided that Wallace had gone daft, just like Wiley. They were all daft. And why? He watched Mrs. Cardwell gaily tuck one of Wallace's blossoms into the rim of her bonnet. She waved and marched along beside her husband down Broadway.

Wallace trudged out of sight. When no one was looking, Griff bent over and quickly scooped up a bruised, fallen petal. He smelled its strange, sweet fragrance, then quickly stuffed the flower petal inside his pocket—terrified that someone might make fun of him.

Once in Chicago, after a long, exhausting train ride in open boxcars, the First Volunteers discovered that they were to be divided. Six companies were to proceed to St. Louis, and four were to travel to Milwaukee. Griff, Wallace, and Wiley were headed with Colonel Dimon by train for St. Louis. The wheels clattered as the train barreled along through the flat Illinois countryside. Griff noticed that their ranks had begun to thin a little. "What happened?" Griff asked Wallace.

"Twenty men deserted in New York. Another dozen vanished in Chicago," Wallace replied matter-of-factly. "They made a poor choice leaving when they did, if you ask me."

Griff looked around to make sure no officer might be listening. "What do you mean?"

"I mean that once we arrive in St. Louis, we're heading north by steamboat to some place on the Missouri River called Fort Rice, Dakota Territory. The river's the fastest, surest route to Fort Benton. Then it's only a short overland trip to the Montana gold fields," Wallace said in a confidential tone of voice. "A man could make a real fortune, if he's clever."

"Gold?" Griff whispered eagerly.

Wallace winked. "You bet. I hear the Montana nuggets are so heavy and so plentiful that a man can barely tote them by himself. Needs a string of mules to carry his new wealth. No use hard soldiering for very long when that kind of easy money can be made. I intend to slip away when the time's right and head to Montana myself. Care to join me? I could use a clever young companion like you."

Griff gulped. The offer sounded good. Perhaps too good. He studied Wallace. Could he trust him? If either of them were caught deserting, they'd be court-martialed. He didn't want to go back to prison. "I'll think about it," Griff whispered.

"Don't think too long. When the time's right, I'm going. Opportunity waits for no man," Wallace warned. His eyes narrowed as he jabbed Griff in the collarbone with a sharp finger. "I know I can count on you to keep our little private conversation a secret."

Griff nodded uneasily. He couldn't tell if Wallace's words were a compliment or a threat.

On August 27, the six remaining companies boarded the *Effie Deans* in St. Louis. Painted white, the various decks of the wooden ship rose from a flat-barge base like some kind of elaborate layered cake on a great platter. The topmost lookout, or pilothouse, had the best view of the river in all directions. This was where the captain stood. Griff found it odd that the pilothouse was sheathed in boiler iron that had been dented with bullet pockmarks. He found the same shrapnel damage in the steamboat's 25-foot-tall stern wheel in the back, or the stern, of the boat. Individual paddles from this wooden wheel hit the water and pushed the boat forward or backward, depending on the direction the wheel was turning.

The *Effie Deans*'s captain was a famous river man rumored to be half-alligator. His name was LaBarge. The swarthy French steamboat crew spoke a strange language that sounded like pigeon-coo to Griff. They wore something called moccasins—odd, low, soft shoes that were made by Indians.

Among the passengers were plenty of boisterous miners. Their tales of gold only made Griff more impatient. The *Effie Deans* chugged along, gaining 45 miles a day. When the steamboat turned upriver into the strongest part of the current, she shook like an old rattlebox. The engine strained, and the smokestack belched sparks. Griff wondered if the *Effie Deans* might shake herself to pieces before they ever reached Fort Rice.

Whenever he could, Griff tried to talk to the miners to find out where they were headed and what they hoped to find. But they all looked at him as if he were a mere stupid, dark-haired child in a soldier's uniform. They wasted his time by regaling him with far-fetched stories about their adventures in St. Louis. Griff held his peace. He knew how to be patient and watch and wait.

He smiled, thinking how his life had changed! Just two weeks ago he was trapped in Virginia, a sitting target for any Confederate sniper. Now here he was aboard a steamboat bound for the fabulous West.

As soon as he was a rich prospector, he'd buy a big brick house with three stairways and a great strong door and plenty of guards for protection. No one would dare enter his house unless invited. He'd never have to be afraid of anyone again. In his kitchen there'd be a long table heaped with good things to eat—clabber, butter, bacon and cornbread, griddle cakes. Upstairs he'd have a room with a soft bed with a thick feather tick. On the bedroom floor would be a row of shoes. A new pair for every day of the week.

Chapter 4

Days dragged by as the *Effie Deans* struggled upstream. It seemed to Griff that the Missouri was the crookedest, longest, muddiest river he had ever laid eyes on. The Pee Dee River, the biggest river he knew back home, was nothing compared to the Missouri for pure thickness. "Too silty to drink, too thin to plow," Wiley said and seemed to think himself very clever.

The shrunken Missouri looked gaunt and sinewy— nothing to be feared. It reminded Griff of a tawny, half-starved stray dog. Long, dry sandbars protruded from the river like ribs. The main current rippled in a ropy movement like lean muscles on a dog's back.

The only remains of the Missouri's terrible power were mangled piles of uprooted trees and shattered limbs hurled on the embankment during the river's high water days.

Boatmen called these piles "rack heaps." April and June, they said, were the only times the river reliably rose high enough for a flat-bottomed steamboat to make the 3,000-mile journey from St. Louis to the distant-most Fort Benton. Two years of drought had left the Missouri's water level lower than ever. The boatmen complained that traveling north against the current in September was nothing short of madness. In some places the river was less than a foot deep.

Nothing could dissuade impatient Colonel Dimon or the raucous gold miners aboard the *Effie Deans*. They seemed bound for glory—no matter what the price.

Griff and the other 600 soldiers were crowded aboard the rattling stern-wheeler with chickens, goats, cows, and horses. The journey seemed to take forever. The Nebraska territory on the left and Iowa farmland on the right crept past at a turtle's pace. Low river-bottoms gave way to open vistas of green prairie that stretched clear to the horizon. Every so often the view was blocked by high, rolling bluffs.

Although the soldiers had become accustomed to the close quarters and monotony of prison, they felt dangerously restless aboard the *Effie Deans* with nothing to do. Some tried to bide their time by playing cards. Some struggled to sleep. Others read books with pages nearly transparent from so much handling. Every day, 30 cords of wood had to be cut along shore to feed the steamboat's hungry boiler. This provided a few daring souls with the opportunity to sneak away after wooding expeditions to "borrow" watermelons from a nearby field. One night near Independence, Missouri, several soldiers dropped silently into the water, waded to shore, and were never seen again.

When he heard about those deserters, Griff became impatient to escape.

"We're still a far piece from Fort Rice," Wallace whispered one evening in early September. He and Griff were both on deck doing guard duty. "You want to walk the whole way to the Wind River gold fields? I'll give you the sign when I'm ready."

That night a full moon rose in the clear night sky. White light danced on dark water and illuminated the ghostly stands of cottonwood along the river's edge. Pale, dry leaves twisted and danced in the wind. Somewhere on board ship a harmonica began to play. A sad, homesick voice sang very softly:

"I wish I was in the land of cotton
Old times there are not forgotten
Look away, look away, look away Dixie Land!
In Dixie Land where I was born—"

"Fall in!" an officer shouted. The music and singing stopped. Lanterns flared. An unexpected roll call was ordered. Men who had been sleeping were jolted off the deck and made to stand at attention. Anyone who did not obey fast enough was forced to spend the rest of the evening on their feet.

"Colonel's nothing but a young puppy," someone muttered.

"Chicken-livered, shoulder-strapped upstart," another hissed.

Griff grumbled but did as he was told. He rubbed his eyes with his fist and said his name.

"We must have discipline. We must have loyalty. Any deserters will face serious consequences," Colonel Dimon said in a high-pitched, trembling voice. He marched back and forth across the cramped deck with his hand on the hilt of his saber. "An example must be set. As your commander, I have the power of life and death over you. Do not make the mistake of underestimating me."

Someone snickered, "Another runaway flown the coop." In the moonlight Griff could see from the soldiers' slack-jawed expressions that they were unimpressed by the colonel's threats.

Rain fell for the next several days as the *Effie Deans* steamed slowly toward Omaha. There were few places aboard ship where the men could keep dry. Complaining became louder than usual. Someone posted a picture near the latrine that looked suspiciously like the colonel in a woman's hat.

One afternoon Wallace approached Griff with a serious face. "Better come and listen to this," Wallace said. He poked Griff, who had been napping under a dripping piece of canvas. "They're court-martialing Dowdy."

"Dowdy?" Griff sputtered as he followed Wallace to the other side of the deck. "What for?"

"Just listen."

Captain Fay, downy-bearded, lisped the charges

brought against Private William C. Dowdy, a brawny, red-haired private who was formerly a blacksmith in Bedford County, Tennessee. " . . . Violation of the 21st Article of War, or absenting himself from his company without leave. And by committing a violation of the 7th Article of War: 'Any officer or soldier who shall begin, excite, cause, or join in, any mutiny, or sedition, in any troop or company in the Service of the United States, or in any party, post, detachment, or guard, shall suffer death or such other punishment as by a court-martial shall be inflicted.' "

"What did he do?" Griff whispered to Wallace.

"They're trying him for saying he'd be damned if he would not take the first opportunity to desert the regiment," Wallace replied. His mouth was a hard, straight line. "Of course, Dimon has no legal right, no authority to try or punish capital offenses. There's only the slightest bit of evidence. One man's word against another's."

Griff swallowed hard. As slowly and quietly as possible, he moved away from Wallace, who seemed to know too much and speak too freely. What if Dimon fingered him next?

After only two days of testimony from a few of Dimon's cronies and a handful of foreign-born soldiers who barely spoke English, Dowdy was found guilty of all charges and was ordered to be executed. "Private Dowdy has had full warning, and after betraying the confidence of his officers and inciting his comrades to unlawful acts, can expect no sympathy of officers or men," Colonel Dimon announced.

Griff and the other men listened in disbelief. No one spoke as the steamboat chugged past Omaha and pulled to shore at the first convenient landing place on the Iowa side of the river. The last landing bell rang, and the boat lay snubbed to the bank. The afternoon heat felt oppressive as the anchor was lowered and planks were run ashore. Griff was among the grave-digging detail that shouldered shovels. He felt too afraid to speak or meet anyone's glance as he slowly helped dig a trench in the soft, muddy ground. Drums rolled a sad, slow beat. Six companies marched off the boat and stood in a square with the grave forming the fourth side. Four men lowered a hastily built wooden coffin into the fresh grave.

Next came 22-year-old Dowdy in manacles. His face was flushed, and his blue eyes seemed terrified as he kneeled beside the open grave. The firing squad marched into position. Colonel Dimon checked his pocket watch. He gave the signal. At precisely three o'clock, musket fire rang out, and Dowdy fell face-first into his own coffin.

Griff gripped the shovel to keep his hands from shaking as Colonel Dimon read from the Bible in a high-pitched voice. Wiley mumbled his own prayer. The other men, ashen-faced and silent, turned and marched back up the gangway to the ship. Griff and the other men in his detail set to work closing the coffin and filling the grave. When they were finished and about to reboard, Griff could not help himself. He leaned against a tree with one hand and vomited into the fallen leaves.

For the next several miles, anyone who watched the *Effie Deans* from shore might have thought the steamboat was being operated by ghosts—so silent were the decks. The boiler rumbled. Smoke belched from the smokestack. The stern wheel splashed and turned. But no one on board spoke. No one dared.

Miles later, the scenery began to change. The river twisted and turned. Wind blew across the plains and slammed the *Effie Deans* into snags and sandbars. When the boat wouldn't budge, the crew had to tie lines to a distant tree—if they could find one—and pull the boat forward by taking up the line with a small steam-powered winch. When that didn't work, Griff and the others disembarked. The steamboat used two "grasshopper poles" in front, which were lowered into the sand to help lift the boat and actually pull the craft forward. Each time the boat inched upriver, the poles were reset. The boat crawled north.

Slowly, time passed. At the mouth of the Little Sioux River, the soldiers went ashore and cut 15 cords of dry wood. Griff watched a noisy black *V* of geese flying south and wished he could join them. Farther upriver, a small group of Indians in tattered clothing from the Omaha Reservation stood on shore and signaled to the steamboat to come in. Captain LaBarge kept going. Every delay meant that the boat might meet with shallower water upstream.

The farther north the steamboat moved, the more the country began to change. Fewer and fewer trees dotted the shoreline. Whenever a stand of cottonwood with clattering yellow leaves were spotted, the steamboat stopped, and a wood-cutting expedition went ashore. Cold wind blew down from the north at night and made Griff shiver. There was another reason the boat was in such a hurry. Once winter set in, the river would freeze solid. Some of the crew members told Griff that nobody in their right mind would winter in the upper reaches of the Missouri.

Griff hoped they were only trying to scare him.

When the boat passed the Jim River, the bluffs on either side rose up bare of timber and grass. And Griff began to wonder what kind of country he was entering. Up ahead, the biggest town in the territory was Yankton, just 18 months old and nothing more than a bunch of cottonwood cabins and tents clustered on the high, rolling prairie. This would be the last real town they would pass. The men were anxious to make a visit, but Colonel Dimon ordered everyone to stay on board.

At night the steamboat anchored at Bonhomme Island, seeking protection among the few trees from cold, howling wind that raced down the river. Waves rocked the ship. Now they were more than 1,100 miles from St. Louis. With every passing mile, Griff had the feeling that he was leaving every trace of civilization. He wondered what lay beyond the barren bluffs that formed a kind of wall on each side of the river? How far would a man have to walk to reach another living soul?

To pass the time, Griff surveyed the shore for animals. A few antelope or perhaps a herd of deer would sometimes dart into view and quickly vanish. Griff saw no buffalo, much to his disappointment. He wished he could bring down one of the great shaggy beasts that he had heard so much about. Soldiers were occasionally allowed to take shots at flocks of geese and ducks.

They passed the mouth of the Niobrara River and made their way past the desolate Bijou Hills. Griff scanned the strange bald cliffs and thought he saw someone staring down at them.

"You see that?" Griff asked Wiley, who stood beside him.

Wiley looked up and peered in the distance. "Rock," he replied.

"No, it's a man digging."

Wiley's expression screwed up into a thoughtful expression. "Maybe an Indian looking for something to eat. I hear they're so starved they scrape the ground for wild roots to eat. One of the fellows told me buffalo's been scared off. Indians' crops on the reservation failed this year, and government rations ain't come through."

"Hunger will cause a man to do almost anything," Griff murmured. He recalled the gnawing, empty feeling he had endured at Point Lookout.

Wiley gazed up and down the river at the steep bluffs. "Indians could be thick as blackbirds up there, and we wouldn't see nary a one till it was too late to duck for cover."

Griff nodded nervously and moved to the other side of the boat.

Chapter 5

On September 27, five miles below the mouth of the White Earth River, the *Effie Deans* wedged herself into a sandbar and went aground for the last time. When Captain LaBarge sent a scouting party upstream, they came back with bad news. The water was even shallower up ahead. Colonel Dimon announced that they would march the last 272 miles overland to Fort Rice. Griff and the others unloaded the ammunition and supplies on shore. Forty miles upriver was the Crow Creek Agency, where Colonel Dimon told the men they would buy a few extra wagons and horses, if any were available.

With great effort, the men hauled their belongings and supplies up the embankment and over the steep bluffs. "Don't look good to me," said Wiley, who was first to hoist his heavy pack to the top.

Griff had never in his life seen anything so barren and desolate as the unforgiving land he beheld when the regiment crawled onto the Dakota plains. Not a single tree could be seen for miles. Massive clouds muscled across an enormous sky. The blue space overhead was so vast that it seemed to press down on his chest and suck all the breath from his body. Watching the endless, dry, yellow-brown grass roll and shift made him feel dizzier than he'd felt floating on the ocean.

Occasionally, hills could be seen in the lonely distance. He heard no birds, no other animals. The only other signs of life were the hurtling mobs of grasshoppers that leaped underfoot as the men trudged through the bone-dry grass. Cold, biting wind howled, picked up dust, and flung it into the men's eyes and teeth and hair. Wind hissed and stole the men's hats and hurled them out of reach. Wind pushed and shoved the men so that they had to bend nearly double to make any progress.

Colonel Dimon and the other officers pranced along on horses that they had transported on the steamboat. They did not have to walk and eat dust like the rest of the men. Griff watched the officers on horses pass by. *Do they really know where they're going?* The enormity of the place and the sky and the relentless wind made Griff feel small and insignificant and lost.

"See her?" Wiley said in a low, happy voice.

"Who?" Griff grumbled as he trudged along.

"Mrs. Cardwell," Wiley jutted his thumb. "She's

45

walking along beside her husband. Jolly as can be. Refuses to ride one of the horses. How do you like that?"

Griff did not reply. He thought it ridiculous to walk when a person could ride. The other men were impressed. They cheered heartily when she passed by. Griff grimaced. *Fools*, he thought.

After a cold, wet night in a hailstorm without any protection, the company quickly lost its good humor and began to complain. Rations were cut to two hard crackers, two tablespoons of coffee grounds and sugar mixed, and a small portion of salt pork for the day. On the third day of their march, Griff and the others wearily arrived at the Crow Creek Agency, which was nothing more than a stockade of 12-foot-tall pickets of cedar surrounding a village of tepees. Colonel Dimon managed to locate and purchase a few ox-drawn wagons.

"Would you look there?" Griff said to Wiley. He had never been so close to real Indians before and felt amazed and a little frightened. The Crow Creek Indians wore blankets around their shoulders. They did not seem particularly fierce. Their hair was decorated with feathers and beads. Some wore hide leggings. Their dirty faces were striped with grease and paint, and they seemed intent on trading moccasins for tobacco and shining brass buttons. Meanwhile, the Indian children ran around nearly buck naked and didn't seem to notice the cold.

After three days at the agency, the men were marched north again past barren, bell-shaped hills. They camped at

Soldier's Creek. Before dawn the next day, they marched toward Medicine Creek. Tall, dry grass muttered in bone-chilling wind. Crushed grass crackled underfoot. "Sounds like shattered glass in a deserted house," Wallace said as he marched along beside Griff. Griff walked around a vicious tuft of prickly pear. "Dang thorny stuff."

"You've been avoiding me," Wallace said.

Griff shrugged. Since Dowdy's execution, talking to Wallace seemed too dangerous. "I've not been feeling well," Griff lied.

"You and many others," Wallace said. He shifted his pack to his other shoulder. "Hope you didn't eat any of that fry bread back in Crow Creek. I have heard from reliable sources that those red-skinned heathens fry their dough in dog fat."

Griff felt his stomach lurch. He *had* tried the fry bread. It was greasy and tough. He decided to change the subject. "When will we get to Fort Rice?"

"After we reach Fort Sully tomorrow, it's nearly one hundred and seventy miles north. There's scarcely any wood or water between the two forts. Some of the boys say they think Dimon's lost his senses the way he's taking a shortcut across the Big Bend. Sometimes I wonder if we'll ever make it. Do you?"

Griff did not reply. Was this some kind of trap? "Don't have no opinion," he said in a low voice.

"There's a good soldier!" Wallace laughed harshly. "Once upon a time you had enterprise and spunk. What happened to you?"

Griff shrugged and felt glad when Wallace marched away.

Hours passed. Griff's shoulders ached from carrying his heavy pack. His mouth was dry, and there was very little water to be had until the regiment stopped to camp at nightfall. When he tried to find Wiley, he discovered that Wiley had an acute stomachache and could not even sit up without much effort. He bounced along in one of the wagons with four other groaning, sick men.

"I'll keep an eye on your belongings for you," Griff volunteered. "Don't trust these North Carolina boys for a minute."

Wiley thanked him profusely.

Griff slung Wiley's pack on his back and considered that he'd have first pick of Wiley's worldly possessions if he keeled over for good.

The next day, Griff heard that Wiley had made a remarkable recovery after Mrs. Cardwell stopped at his wagon and talked to him at some length while she walked along beside the other troops.

On October 7, the regiment arrived at Fort Sully, a crude place with earth-roofed barracks and an unimpressive picket stockade. The windowless buildings had dirt floors and decaying cottonwood log walls that harbored swarms of bedbugs and rats. In spite of their primitive conditions, Fort Sully's men from the Sixth Iowa Cavalry hooted when they saw the First Volunteers stumble inside the palisade.

"Still look like seedy Rebs—even in your Yankee clothes!" one shouted.

"Whitewashed Rebs!" another joined in.

A few boys from Virginia pulled up their sleeves and were about to come to blows when the captain rode up and broke up the fight before it started. "Save your blows for the Indians," he ordered.

"Indians don't take no prisoners," one of the Iowa Cavalrymen said to Griff as he passed.

Griff paused. "You been to Fort Rice?"

The Iowa soldier spit and nodded. "You should know that the red men don't follow regular rules of war. They kill and chop up every man they capture." He made a strange motion with his finger at his greasy hair. "Slice a piece of hair and scalp to take for a souvenir. Fort Rice's a good place to lose your hair, young fellow. Listen to me."

Griff nervously examined the soldier. His long, sunburned face was lean. A scar ran from the corner of one eye to his chin. He wore buckskin trousers and soft moccasins. His hair was long and tied in back with a piece of dirty rawhide. Here was someone who had been to the distant places Griff was going. He knew the territory. "How far from Fort Rice to the Montana gold fields?" Griff whispered.

The Iowa soldier laughed. "Ain't the right question. Right question is how fast can you move with a bunch of young bucks on your tail, riding fast as the wind on small, nimble pintos that don't need no water, no grass for miles and miles."

Griff's shoulders slumped forward.

During the next week, the only water to be found was in stagnant pools. Four men who drank the water died and were buried in the dry, desolate hills. Griff sipped the last of his fresh water carefully. He had no intention of dying after he'd come this far.

"Help me look for firewood," Wiley told Griff one afternoon when they reached Beaver Creek. Wiley seemed completely revived. They both took their guns and headed into a ravine outside the regiment's encampment. "Looks like an old orchard on a worn-out farm back home."

Griff nodded. He bent over to pick up a rotten branch of sagebrush, then froze. "Wiley?" he said in a tremulous voice.

"Rattler? Don't move. I'll kill it," Wiley whispered and pointed his gun.

"Ain't no snake," Griff said and pointed. "Look."

Lying among the rocks and prickly pear were the unmistakable bleached shapes of crushed skulls. Human skulls.

"Think they're white folks?" Wiley said hoarsely.

Speechless, Griff stumbled backward. *They kill every man they capture*, the Iowa cavalryman's words echoed in his ears. "Let's get out of here," he said.

They scrambled back to camp as quickly as they could.

Early in the morning of October 17, the weary regiment finally came to a halt. On the west side of the Missouri River, they had their first look at Fort Rice. A shout went up among the men. "What a cry of joy as we view our new home's unfinished battlements!" Wallace said over the din. "As joyous are we as the relics of Xenophon's ten thousand when they beheld the sea whose waters laved their homes."

Wiley looked at Wallace as if he'd lost his mind. "What?"

Wallace grinned and slapped the big man on his back. "Poetry. Pure poetry."

A ferry carried the men across to the fort. Wearily, Griff and the others surveyed their new home. The fort was unfinished—nothing more than a pile of green cottonwood and a few crude huts that might sleep no more than four companies of men. The palisade of helter-skelter timber had been finished on only two sides. A group of tepees and huts less than a half-mile away nestled in the bluffs.

"Who are they, sir?" Griff asked Captain Fay as he passed.

"No one for you to trouble with. They're simply *waglukka*, loafers who hang around the fort begging for handouts," Fay replied.

"He means to say," whispered another soldier, "they're friendly, drunk Indians."

The bugler blew a signal. The regiment assembled for an announcement. "Construction will begin immediately," Colonel Dimon announced to the assembled men. "We will assign details to cut timber and operate two small

sawmills. The rest will build barracks and officers'
quarters. Reveille at 6:00 A.M., surgeon's call at 6:15,
breakfast at 6:45, guard mountings at 7:30, dinner at
noon, recall from fatigue at 4:30 P.M., retreat at sundown,
tattoo at 7:45, and taps at 8:00."

"What about drill, sir?" asked a private from Georgia.

"No drill until necessary buildings complete," Captain
Fay replied.

"Sir, what about Sabbath, sir?" Wiley said.

"Sunday will include prayers, inspection, and dress
parade."

Someone grumbled, "No rest for the wicked."

"All right, men. Get to work," Captain Fay announced.

Griff turned to join the men who were trudging
toward the sawmill near the river. He spotted someone out
of the corner of his eye. A curious face peered at him from
beneath a wagon.

When he looked again, the face was gone. As he and
the other men marched down the bluff to the sawmill, a
chubby young girl—perhaps 10 years old—with long dark
braids, darted between the rocks and shrubs. Boldly, she
walked behind Griff.

"Indian's following you," Wiley said and gave Griff a
nudge in the ribs.

Griff frowned and made a motion with his hand for
the girl to go away and leave him alone. Instead she smiled
and shadowed him all the way to the sawmill at the
bottom of the bluff.

Chapter 6

All day, Griff worked at the sawmill. The mechanism itself was crude, nothing more than a long-handled saw for two men to cut the green cottonwood logs in half. The sun felt warm. Since they were out of the wind at the bottom of the bluff, he was glad when their foreman said they could stop and rest for a while. Griff sat on the bank of the river and watched a pair of swans flap noisily overhead. Their enormous white wings beat the air. *Whump-whump-whump.* They were going far, far away from this place. *Lucky*, thought Griff.

He was so busy watching the birds that he did not at first notice the barefoot girl. Expertly, she picked her way over sharp rocks and around thorny bushes. She carried a great bunch of deep purple plums inside the skirt of her dirty gingham dress. Her legs were dusty and covered with mosquito bites. She wore her dark hair parted in the middle. Two scruffy braids hung to her shoulders. Her black eyes studied Griff with an amused expression that he found disconcerting. Every so often she took a plum from her skirt and popped it into her mouth.

Griff decided that she must be one of the worthless *waglukka*. She probably only wanted some handout—maybe some sugar or tobacco. He decided to ignore her.

She smiled and sat down beside him. With an explosive noise, she spit out three plum pits right in a row. Griff looked away from the girl's sticky purplish face. She was even worse than the filthy children who lived in shacks up in the pine barrens back home. She was an Indian.

The girl handed him a plum. At first, he waved her offer away and shook his head. After she persisted a second and then a third time, he finally took the wizened little plum. Gingerly, he wiped it on his filthy shirt as if to remove all contamination. He bit into the plum's thin skin. His face puckered up.

The girl laughed uproariously at his expression.

In as manly a manner as possible, he swallowed. Then he coughed. "You call that a plum?" he sputtered. "In Carolina we got papaws taste sweeter than that."

"Where is Carolina?" the girl asked and popped another plum in her mouth.

Griff was so taken aback that she could speak English that he didn't know what to say. "Long, long way from here." He took another savage bite, then spit the pit too.

He couldn't believe he was talking about home with this disgusting girl. He never talked about where he came from to anybody.

"How do you like *here?*" She offered him another plum.

He examined a worm hole in the plum. "Wind blows too much like pouring cold water down a fellow's back to suit me."

She laughed again and slapped her leg in a very unladylike manner.

"What's so funny?" he demanded angrily. He could see that the other men were watching them now and smiling in a way that he knew would mean trouble when he got back to the fort.

"*You* are funny," she said, grinning. "Just like Sam. What they call your name?"

Griff sighed. He didn't want to tell her his name. He wanted to get up and walk away, up the hill where he might be safe again. But he knew she would just follow him and keep asking. "Griff," he said slowly.

The girl wrinkled up her nose. "Crazy name. Gruff."

"Griff," he said with irritation. "John Griffith Allen. That's the whole thing."

"Griff of Carolina, now I tell you my name. Ma calls me Alma. Pa calls me *Cheewink*. Grandmother says my name *Ma ga si ca*. Sam calls me Pest."

Griff decided Sam had the right idea. "Sam one of the soldiers?"

Alma shook her head sadly. "Sam is my brother." She looked down the river. "I sing Brave Heart Song for him. He is your age. Gone to the Black Robes and brick houses."

Griff looked at her in confusion. What was she talking about?

She pulled a piece of twisted metal from a little rawhide bag tied around her neck. Reverently, she examined the rusty shape. "Sam give me this."

"What is it?"

She shrugged. "Part of something from Wagon Wheel Bluff. Secret place. I take you there sometime."

Griff did not want to go anywhere with this girl. He took a deep breath. He laced and unlaced his fingers. "Well, been a pleasure talking to you, Alma," he said and stood up. "Thanks for the plums."

Suddenly, a loud woman's voice called down the bluff. Griff shielded his eyes with one hand and looked up. He saw an Indian woman motioning to Alma and shouting in some language he did not understand. Alma jumped to her feet and ran up the bluff, not even turning to say goodbye.

The other men, who were relaxing closer to the river turned and laughed. "Got a *bois brule* sweetheart already, Griff?" one joked. "Half-breed name means 'burnt wood,' just like the mixed color of mulattos back home."

"Kind of young for you, ain't she?" another said.

Griff blushed and clenched his jaw. He knew the

others just wanted to see if they could make him mad enough to fight. He wasn't going to give them that pleasure.

"I'd take care if I was you, Griff," the foreman said in an exaggerated manner. "Her pa's Major Charles Galpin."

"Who's that?" Griff asked, hoping his voice sounded as if he did not care.

"White fur trader and fort sutler. Powerful man if you want to get your hand on supplies in this godforsaken place."

"What kind of supplies you talking about?" Griff asked.

"Gold pans and picks. Salt pork and beans. You know my meaning?" the foreman grinned. "Well, gentlemen, I guess we'd better get back to our labors."

Griff dusted off the back of his dirty pants and decided that perhaps his encounter with Alma might prove lucky after all.

Late that afternoon, the bugler signaled a stranger's approach. The men grabbed their guns, expecting Indians to burst over the hill. To their surprise instead came a wagon and team. Soldiers swung open the fort gate, and in galloped a team and wagon driven by a soldier. Sitting in the back seat was a dust-covered figure holding a dust-covered parasol.

The sudden appearance of a visitor caused a great commotion at the fort. The fact that someone arrived overland on the same grueling route they had just taken surprised the soldiers. What was even more shocking was the fact that their visitor was a young woman.

Colonel Dimon, in full dress uniform, marched in precise steps to the wagon. A middle-aged, portly Indian woman with long black braids and a white-fringed doeskin dress hurried along a few steps behind him. At her side was a tall man that Griff vaguely recognized.

The visitor looked down at the crowd of greeters. She collapsed the parasol and gave it a shake. The tall man extended his hand, and the visitor daintily stepped from the wagon. She had a veil over her face, the kind Griff had seen fancy travelers using in New York City. With a swift movement, she removed her veil and bonnet with her gloved hands. Even covered with dust, her beauty was so astonishing that for several moments none of the soldiers spoke. The visitor seemed accustomed to causing a commotion wherever she went and went on chatting in an animated fashion.

Griff wished he could hear what she was saying. He struggled to peer around Wallace and Wiley, who had stepped rudely in front of him. "Handsome brunette," Wallace said, craning his neck for a better look. "Fine black expressive eyes, arched eyebrows, high forehead shaded with natural ringlets of black flowing hair. An aquiline nose, pretty mouth, teeth exquisitely beautiful, and the contour of her face of an oval form. Tall, slender, well-proportioned but very delicate—"

"You finished?" Griff demanded. He pushed Wallace

out of the way to see for himself. Sure enough, the mysterious visitor was quite stunning. Griff, who ordinarily didn't pay much attention to the beauty of the few passing ladies who had ever come in view of the First Volunteers, had to admit that this new arrival was prettier than Mrs. Cardwell, who stood beside her, shaking her hand. The visitor was a sight more attractive than Mrs. Larned, the heavyset, jovial woman who sold the soldiers pies. And next to the older Indian woman, the visitor certainly was far beyond compare.

Griff watched spellbound as the mysterious visitor completed what seemed to be most likely an exchange of greetings and introductions. Then she turned swiftly away from the small group of women who lived in the fort. Confidently, she took Colonel Dimon's arm. Together, they walked toward the only finished house, chatting politely. The tall man and the Indian woman followed them at a respectful distance.

"Dimon's sweetheart?" Wiley mumbled.

Wallace chuckled. "I believe not."

"Who is she then?" Griff said, vexed by Wallace's little guessing games. "Married to one of the other officers?"

Wallace shook his head. "She is not married to anyone, as far as I know. She's a relation of Major Galpin's, I hear. Fresh from convent school in St. Louis." His eyes were dreamy, as if he were thinking about a time long ago and far away. "I was once known as a charming fellow with such refined young ladies."

Wiley guffawed. "Enlisted man ain't got much of a chance up against the likes of the colonel and the other shoulder straps."

Wallace seemed to pay no attention to Wiley's humbug. He turned to Griff and rubbed his hands together. "I propose a wager."

"What kind of wager?" Griff demanded warily.

"I bet fifty Yankee dollars that in the next twenty-four hours you cannot speak to our charming visitor."

Griff sucked in his bottom lip. Fifty Yankee dollars was a lot of money.

"Griff can do it if anybody can," Wiley said confidently. "Griff can do anything."

A broad smile split Wallace's face. He slapped Griff on the back. "Well, what do you say, my good man? Here's my chance to win back all my money from you."

Griff gulped.

"Would you not agree that she was neither bold nor bashful?" Wallace continued. "Her behavior appeared free, unconstrained, and yet remarkably modest. The result, no doubt, of a superior upbringing. I say you'll have to rise very high to meet this challenge, Griff. What's your answer? You have exactly twenty-four hours. Do you think you can do it?"

"Of course," Griff lied. He shook hands with Wallace with as much confidence as he could muster. Deep down, he knew he had as much chance of having a conversation with such a fine young woman as hell freezing over.

That evening at sundown, Griff combed his unruly hair and washed his face. He paced back and forth outside the barracks. Time was wasting away, and he had not a clue how to approach the visitor. Maybe he should just give up. Just give Wallace the $50. Why humiliate himself?

Griff wrapped his wool coat around himself and rubbed his raw, chapped hands together. The chill never seemed to go out of the air. Miserable gray light was all that illuminated the threatening horizon. To Griff's astonishment, something that looked like pale feathers began to fall all around him.

"Skift of snow," said Wiley, who joined him staring up into the heavens. He held out his big hand to catch the dusting of flakes. "I remember snow once up in the Blue Ridge Mountains."

But it was more than just a skift of snow. It snowed all night. The next morning, Griff was amazed to see the transformation of the landscape. Everything was white. Everything was quiet. He had never seen so much snow before in his life, and he was amazed by its softness and the way it muffled sound. He shuffled through the ankle-deep snow toward Wallace, who stared out at the white plains. "What do you think of the snow?" Griff asked.

Wallace turned to him and shook his head sadly. "We are so far outside the land of civilization," he said. "We might as well be in the heart of the Atlantic Ocean. And how is my wager coming? You have precisely seven hours left."

"Don't worry. I'll win the bet," Griff said. He looked out and felt overwhelmed by the distance and the cold and the snow and the awful possibility of losing all his money again. What could he do to avoid giving Wallace all the pay he'd earned as a First Volunteer?

Deep in thought, he wandered across the snow-covered parade grounds. In the muffled quiet he heard something strange. Someone crying. When he walked around behind the sutler's store, he saw Alma digging furiously in the snow. She had a small crude spade. With every shovel of snow, she sniffed loudly and wailed with a high keening noise that made Griff uneasy.

At first he considered pretending he did not see her. What good could come from getting involved? Then he recalled who her father was and what advantages her ability to get inside the store might have for him when he was ready to make his escape. "You sick?" he called to her in what he hoped sounded like a helpful and concerned voice.

Alma looked up at him and wiped her nose with her sleeve. With her blanket around her shoulders she looked exactly like the other *waglukka* children.

"Sick in my heart," she said sadly and picked up something wrapped in a piece of cloth that lay on the ground. "My *Ke-a* is dead. I bury him so maybe he come to life in spring."

Griff wondered who *Ke-a* might be. He came closer as Alma unwrapped the cloth. Inside was a turtle. She traced her finger over the dead animal's smooth patterned shell. "So beautiful. We call his name *Pa-pe-sto-la*. Sharp Nose. And he live with us for three years in special box. Not even the dogs dare touch him. *Pa-pe-sto-la* brave warrior turtle."

Griff scratched his head. Long, long ago, when he was younger even than Alma, he had a mangy coon hound named Jefferson. When Old Jeff died, Griff thought his heart would break. "How did he die?"

"Louisa," Alma said bitterly. She rewrapped the turtle. "She say, 'Behave like lady. Why not you civilized?' I hate her."

Griff tried not to smile. It was true that Alma was not civilized.

"She find *Pa-pe-sto-la* in her bed. She scream and put him outside. Outside! Such stupid. Cold kill him. Anybody know that." She sobbed loud and long.

Griff shifted back and forth. His feet were starting to feel numb. He was hungry for his breakfast, and he wanted to be going, but he hated to see her cry. What should he do? He had no experience comforting anybody. Whenever he got hurt, Ma said, "Get up, fool." His two older brothers, when they had taken any note of his blubbering, liked nothing better than to give him a good, swift kick. Griff shuffled awkwardly in the snow. "Maybe you'll find another turtle next season."

Alma wailed louder.

"What's all this fuss about?"

Someone stepped around the corner of the house. It

was the stranger from yesterday. His $50 bet. She was wearing soft kid gloves and a fur-collared coat and hat that bundled around her pretty face.

"I was just . . . I was just," Griff stammered. His words seemed to be stuck in his throat.

But the young woman paid no attention to Griff. She put her hands on her hips and spoke to Alma in a loud voice. "Get off the ground this instant before you catch the grippe. Do you hear me?"

Alma glared back at her in defiance. She held the turtle tightly and did not move. Then she said something in a language that Griff could not understand.

"I would appreciate it very much if you would speak only in English when I am present. I do not understand a word of your heathen gibberish."

Alma took a deep breath. "You are not my mother."

"If I were," the young woman said in a low voice, "I'd teach you a thing or two, you little savage."

"I'd rather be a savage than someone dead like you." With that, Alma spit on the ground and ran out of sight.

The young woman did not move. She did not bother to try and follow Alma. "What do you think you're staring at?" she said angrily at Griff, as if she had suddenly noticed his presence.

"N-nothing, ma'am," he said. He pulled his battered cap from his head and twisted it.

"You her friend?"

"No," he said hastily.

"Well, don't encourage her," the young woman said. Her angry, flushed face seemed even more beautiful to Griff.

Desperately, he tried to concentrate on his $50 wager with Wallace. He tried to think of something clever to say, but he had so little practice speaking to such a strange, elegant creature. She turned as if about to leave.

"Nice of you—" he blurted desperately.

She turned and looked at him with amused curiosity. "Nice of me?"

"Nice of you for taking an interest in the girl. Civilizing her, I mean," Griff said as quickly as he could.

The young woman turned her back to the biting wind. She held her dainty gloved hands to her collar and frowned. "I have no choice. She is my half-sister."

Before Griff could respond, the young woman vanished inside the nearby tent. He stood speechless with surprise. *Her half-sister?* he thought. *How could it be?*

He puzzled for a moment. She and Alma must have the same father, Major Galpin. Maybe he was married twice. Maybe Louisa's mother was white and pretty and frail, just like Louisa. When his first white wife died, maybe Major Galpin married Alma's mother, the Indian.

Satisfied with his explanation, Griff took a deep breath. In spite of the bitter cold, he felt strangely warm. He'd won the bet. And best of all, he knew her name. *Louisa.* The most lovely name he had ever heard.

Chapter 7

Step right up, boys. No need to shove," Mrs. Julia Larned bellowed as she waved her rolling pin in the air. She and her husband had been on their way to the Montana gold fields when their wagon train was attacked by Indians. They were among the lucky survivors who rushed back to Fort Rice.

Griff scanned the line of soldiers that snaked from the Larneds' fragrant-smelling tent to the other side of the parade grounds. With rations cut nearly in half and no new food supply deliveries by boat to be made from the States until spring, Mrs. Larned's independent bakery business was booming.

"Got to spend our own money to fill our stomachs," a private said in a loud voice. "Anything new on the menu, ma'am?"

"Same as usual," Mrs. Larned said and wiped her

plump hands on her apron. "Pies: supply limited, quality common to fair, no spices but little shortening, price thirty cents."

Some of the soldiers laughed. "And what about cakes?" one asked.

"Common ginger and molasses, lightweight, price fifty cents a dozen." She smiled and handed another customer a small, crusty pie, which had a dab of sugar and a transparent, shriveled slice of dried apple wedged inside. "Don't forget we got bread but little done, two slices for ten cents; biscuits, seventy-five cents a dozen; boiled rice, ten cents a saucerful; boiled beans with no meat, twenty-five cents a plate. I know you boys brought nearly twenty thousand dollars when you marched up here. Can't one of you afford a bit of butter?"

The soldiers groaned and hooted. With only one milk cow in the whole fort, the price of butter had skyrocketed to nearly $1.50 a pound.

"Hey!" Griff called when he finally spied Wallace and Wiley. Beaming with jubilation, he hurried to Wallace and whispered, "You owe me fifty dollars. Pay up. I talked to her just like I said I would."

Wallace frowned. "I believe you are obfuscating."

"What?" Griff demanded. He scowled and rolled up his sleeves. "Never did such a thing."

"I believe you are purposefully bewildering me, dear fellow. Tut tut, don't get hot under the collar. I need proof before I part with my money."

"Proof!" Griff exclaimed. When he saw a few fellows in

line staring at him, he lowered his voice and said, "That
wasn't part of the deal. You bet fifty dollars that I wouldn't
talk to her. Well, I did. I can even tell you her name.
Louisa. There, how do you like that?"

"It must have been a scintillating conversation if her
name was all that you found out about her," Wallace said
and glanced at his gold pocket watch. "Were there any
witnesses?"

"Witnesses?"

"People who saw you talking together."

"Just the girl, Alma."

Wallace sniffed. "She's an Indian. She doesn't count."

Griff's eyes narrowed. He knew that Wallace did not
want to admit he was beaten and have to pay up on his
reckless bet. Griff was tired of Wallace treating him like an
ignorant up-country fool. "Double the bet and I'll give
you all the proof you need."

Wallace gulped. "Double it?"

Wiley chuckled. "You afeared, Wallace?"

"Certainly not," Wallace said, then turned to Griff.
"I'll even give you extra time, just so there are no hard
feelings. You have sixteen hours to demonstrate yourself
the winner. Find a respectable witness who sees you in
conversation, or provide something in writing directly
from the fair hand of our mysterious visitor. And I'll
double my wager."

Just as Griff shook hands with Wallace to seal the deal,
a shout rang out from the block house. "Mail's coming!"

called the guard. He stood in the crude, half-built platform that served as the fort's lookout.

Wallace rushed off with the other soldiers who had abandoned their places in line. They wanted to be first to meet the horseback rider carrying letters and newspapers from the outside world.

"Come back here, boys!" Mrs. Larned called to her retreating customers. Her flushed, flour-smeared face sagged with disappointment until she noticed Griff and Wiley. "What'll you have?"

"Cake for me, ma'am," Wiley said and licked his lips.

She handed Wiley a small brown square of dry, crumbling cake. "My own special recipe I brought from Minnesota. What'll you have, son?"

Wiley nudged Griff, who was busy watching the soldiers scrambling for their mail. "Don't pay no mind to my friend's manners, ma'am," Wiley apologized to Mrs. Larned. "He's not usually so rude. Are you, Griff?"

Griff kept staring in the distance, deep in thought. How was he ever going to find a witness or come up with written proof? He doubted that Louisa would ever speak to him again.

Mrs. Larned examined Griff and murmured to Wiley, "How come he's not rushing for the mail like the others?"

Wiley shrugged. "My friend never gets any letters. Never writes any either. Do you, Griff?"

Something in writing, Griff thought. He turned to Wiley. He grinned like a fool.

"Griff, don't take what I said wrong," Wiley said and then gobbled a bite of cake. "Maybe one day your folks will—"

"Thanks for the idea," Griff interrupted. Before Wiley could answer, Griff hurried away. He did not have a moment to lose.

After much searching, he found Alma behind one of the tents. She rolled a hoop a little way across the cleared ground. With one quick movement, she threw a spear inside the moving target. When she noticed that Griff was watching her, she smiled with delight. "Play with me."

"I'm in a hurry." He looked over his shoulder.

"Everyone's always in hurry," Alma said and pouted. "No one will play."

Griff studied her stubborn expression. He knew she wouldn't help him if she were in a bad mood. "All right. What's your game called?"

"Shooting the Buffalo. When I go to Grandmother, my cousins show me. Good practice for hunting. You ever hunt buffalo?"

Griff shook his head. "I used to hunt ducks in the fall back in—"

"Carolina," she chimed in proudly. "I remember."

"That's right." He tapped his foot, eager to change the subject. "Throwing that thing doesn't look hard." He took the spear and threw it just as Alma sent the hoop spinning. The spear fell far short of the target.

"I show you," Alma said. She shot the spear right

70

through the moving hoop. She jumped and clapped. "You try again."

Not wishing to fail twice in front of a girl so much younger than he was, he tried concentrating with all his might. He rolled the hoop, aimed, and threw the spear. The spear merely knocked the hoop over.

"Almost!" Alma said.

Griff felt surprised by her generous encouragement. He tried again and was pleased to see that this time the spear went right inside the hoop.

Alma cheered. "When ice comes on river I teach you to slide on buffalo ribs. Spin very fast. In spring we play Throw At Each Other with Mud and Knocking the Ball Game. Know how?"

Griff shook his head. He had never had time for games when he was younger. Pa always had so many chores for him to do. After his two older brothers joined up and went to war, Griff was responsible for all the milking, plowing, and fence building. Some evenings he was so exhausted that he fell asleep eating his bowl of gruel.

"You not know much for *waiscu*," Alma said and laughed.

"What's a *waiscu?*" he demanded.

"White person. *Waiscu* means white person. Sometimes my Grandmother tells me, 'If you not good, waiscu will get you.' When it is *Campashawik*, Cherry Ripening Moon, I go to her village. She teaches me to make moccasins, scrape buffalo hide. Many important things. Her name means Proud Walking. What is your grandmother name?"

Griff shrugged. He couldn't remember which grandmother had moved to Texas with his cousins or died long ago.

"You *must* have grandmother," Alma said with authority. "Who took care of you when you were little baby and almost fell in fire? Who sings you songs and tells you stories?"

"Nobody," Griff replied with irritation. "I think my grandmothers went up the spout before I was born."

"Up spout? What that?"

"That means they died. I don't really want to talk about it," he said brusquely. Why did Alma always make him feel so edgy? She was just a little girl. She didn't know what she was saying.

"I'm sorry for you," she said in a somber voice.

"Sorry?" Griff said, thoroughly insulted. "Why should *you* feel sorry for me?"

"Grandmothers up the spout can't tell you about cici man and the owl who steals children. Griff of Carolina, you are like lone wolf cub with nobody to teach you."

His face felt flushed and hot with anger. "See here now, do you know where your sister Louisa is? Do you think you could take me to her?"

Alma sniffed as if Louisa's very name were odorous. "She says I am her sister. I do not call her my *tanke*. Why do you want to talk to *her*? Why you not play with me instead?"

Griff sighed. "I have to ask Louisa a favor and I need your help. The rider's leaving soon to take the mail south. I want to send a letter to my . . . to my mother. Do you think Louisa might help me write it?"

"You not know how to write?"

Griff shook his head with embarrassment.

"You not know how to read?"

He shook his head again.

"Me too," Alma replied happily. "I can't read. I can't write. I don't care. Pa and Ma say, 'You go to school in St. Louis.' I don't want to go to those brick houses and Black Robes. They make you dead. Suck away your spirit."

Griff looked up at the sun. He knew the afternoon was disappearing, and he did not want to lose the bet. "Please will you help me ask your sister?" he pleaded.

Alma studied Griff. "Then you do something for me?"

"Anything."

"Go to Wagon Wheel Bluff."

"All right. Fine," he said hurriedly. "Now can we find Louisa?"

Alma took Griff's hand, which made him feel very foolish. He hoped nobody saw him. "You are my *kola*," she said to him as she led him to her family's tent.

"What's *kola?*" he demanded nervously.

She beamed up at him. "Friend."

"I reckon," he said, perplexed as ever.

As it turned out, Louisa seemed quite happy to oblige Griff's request. She quickly dismissed Alma, whom she said was far too dirty to be indoors. Reluctantly, Alma retreated outside the tent.

"Sit here," Louisa instructed Griff. He took a seat at one of the two chairs at the rough-hewn table. She placed two pieces of fresh paper, a pen, and a bottle of ink on the table.

Furtively, Griff looked around. The tent was small and clean. There were two cots at one side and a buffalo robe rolled up against one canvas wall. The floor was made from rough boards, and a small tin stove burning dried cottonwood struggled to keep the space warm. Hanging from a string near a wash basin was a picture of Jesus with a golden crown. His face was very pale and his hair was very yellow.

Griff felt terrified sitting alone so close to Louisa, whose scent reminded him of Mrs. Cardwell's crushed flower petal. *If only the other boys could see me now!* he thought. He stared at the picture of Jesus to keep himself from looking at Louisa, who seemed to nearly blind him with her beauty.

"What do you want to say to your mother?" She tapped the end of the pen on the table.

For a moment, Griff was struck dumb. He couldn't remember his mother's face. He couldn't recall her voice or hardly anything about her. "Tell her howdy."

"Howdy?" Louisa said and shook her head with disgust. "That is no way to start a proper letter. This is how a letter should begin: 'Dear Mother: It is with pleasure that I take my pen in hand to let you know that I am well. I hope these lines may reach you in due time and find you enjoying the same blessing. . . .' "

"That's right pretty," he said in a small voice.

"Sister Mary Margaret taught us that. She said I had the most beautiful penmanship at convent school. What else would you like to tell your mother?"

Griff drummed his fingers on his knee. He felt terrified. "Say I joined the First U.S. Volunteers, and I am in Dakota. We ain't got enough to eat lest the hunting detail bring back some game and don't get ambushed."

Louisa sat up very straight and scowled at the paper. " 'We ain't got' is not proper. You mean 'we have not.' "

Dumbfounded, Griff glanced at her. What was she talking about?

"Shouldn't you tell your mother that you miss her? When was the last time you were home?"

Griff bit his lip. "Can't recall exactly." He gulped. "How about this? 'I have got on as smooth as ever you saw, but I want to be at home mighty bad.' " He knew it wasn't true, but he was pleased to see the way Louisa smiled for the first time as she quickly scratched pen to paper. "Then end up with, 'From your son, Griff.' "

"There's still quite a bit of paper left. It's a sin to waste it. Tell her some news."

Griff frowned. He only needed a little writing in Louisa's hand to win his bet with Wallace. "All right. Say, 'Weather has been boisterous windy.' "

A faint grin passed across her face. She wrote some more.

Encouraged, he continued, " 'Last week boats come in with one hundred seventy miners from Virginia City. They have been one month on the way and had a cold, rough time. I hear plenty of news about the gold mines but little that I can put confidence in.' "

When Louisa was finished, she looked up and said, "You seem very interested in gold."

Griff felt his heart beating very fast. How had she figured out that he planned to run away?

"Gold has caused many souls terrible misery," she continued. "I believe that good works—not wealth—are the swiftest way to enter into heaven. That is why I am helping you write this letter. You are an ignorant, illiterate individual who may one day see the light and be saved. I may only be eighteen years old, but I am very wise to the ways of salvation."

"Thank you, ma'am," Griff said. Now he knew her age. Nearly three years older than he was. A mature young woman. Not like those simpering, irritating girls back home. With renewed awe, he watched her finish the letter. Then he obediently signed his name with an X, the same way he did when he had enlisted. He took the precious $100 letter, folded it, and tucked it inside his pocket. "Hope you get where you're fixing to go."

"I hope you do too," she replied piously.

For a moment, Griff caught a glimpse of Louisa's

practicality. He felt surprised. Louisa did not do anything that did not benefit her in some way. *Neither do I*, he thought, *neither do I.*

"*Mi cunk she?*" someone called from outside the tent. The flap opened, and in stepped The-Eagle-Woman-That-All-Look-At. Griff was surprised to see Major Galpin's wife, a full-blooded Teton Lakota. Unlike other white men's Indian spouses, who were disdainfully called brevet-wives, Eagle Woman was respected in the fort wherever she went. She was Colonel Dimon's most skilled and trusted interpreter.

"Afternoon, ma'am," Griff said.

Eagle Woman smiled at him and raised her hand in a traditional Lakota greeting. When Louisa saw her do this, she frowned. "Must you speak that primitive language and make those barbaric signs in my presence?"

Eagle Woman's smile quickly faded. "*Mi cunk she—*"

"In English!" Louisa commanded.

"My daughter," Eagle Woman said softly. "It has been sixteen long years since I have seen you. Please forgive me if I do not please you. May we not always be strangers?"

Louisa rose and looked at Griff with a cold glance. Griff felt completely baffled. *Daughter?*

"I think you should be going now," Louisa told Griff.

He stumbled toward the door. "Thank you, ma'am," he murmured to Louisa. Then he turned to Eagle Woman and quickly added, "Evening, ma'am."

He hurried away from the tent, where he could still

hear the murmur of the women's unhappy voices. He felt embarrassed at what he had witnessed. *Does anyone else know?*

When he reached his makeshift barracks, he paused for a moment to listen to the bugle signaling the end of the day. To the west, the clouds slowly changed from gold to bronze to dull red. A biting breeze tossed sawdust and sand and dirt skyward. He hugged his elbows tightly against himself and tried to steady his thoughts by concentrating on what seemed familiar. Taps. Sunset. The wind.

No matter how hard he tried, he could not believe what he had just seen and heard. Alma and Louisa shared the same mother—not the same father. Louisa was a *bois brule*.

Wallace's words rang in Griff's ears. *She's an Indian. She doesn't count.*

Chapter 8

Griff collected his hundred-dollar wager from Wallace. But he never told him what he had learned about Louisa. And he never sent his letter to his mother. Instead, he kept it hidden with his other most precious belongings between two cottonwood logs in the wall of the barracks. He wondered if Louisa had put a bewitching spell on him. He decided to stay as far away from her as possible. He tried very hard not to think of her.

Days dragged by, each one colder than the last. Wind chased snow across the frozen, sleeping surface of the river. When Griff complained to Mrs. Larned that he felt as frozen as the Missouri, she told him that he should never settle in Minnesota. "Long winters there too," she said. The cold never seemed to bother her. The only thing that dampened her spirits was a rule sent out by the company's surgeon forbidding the sale of pies. "He's trying to blame my cooking for the eight deaths from chronic diarrhea," she told Griff.

At the end of November, Griff was assigned to help guard hunters who attempted to shoot at anything that might make a meal. It was a blustery day with high winds and steadily dropping temperatures. Griff stood with his gun and scanned the nearby hills for any sign of Indians. He wondered what foolish Indian would leave a warm tepee to creep out on the year's coldest day yet. As he blew on his numb hands, he heard a loud crack. At first he felt convinced that it must be one of the hunters. Suddenly, four men came tearing over the hill on horseback. Following hot on their heels were a dozen screaming Indians on swift ponies.

Griff couldn't budge. He felt as if he were in a dream, and his legs refused to work.

"Get inside!" shouted the men being pursued. "Back to the fort!"

The Indians yipped louder. Griff ran to his bony horse that had been picketed nearby. Clumsily, he swung into the saddle. The old horse seemed to sense danger and took off at a surprisingly fast gallop toward the fort.

Griff heard bullets whiz past. He clutched his gun with one hand but did not have the presence of mind to load and shoot. He bent forward and held tight to the horse as it took him at a hard gallop. He bounced in the saddle. The guard swung open the gate. Already the howitzer was being trained on the Indians. *Boom! Boom!* In the cold, the exploding shells seemed even louder.

Griff could barely stop his horse as it tore inside the fort. He was aware only that he was still alive. He had been gripping so tightly, he didn't notice that his cramped hand had nearly frozen to the metal gun barrel.

"Positions!" someone shouted. Firing began. But the Indians had already turned and ridden out of range.

Two men were wounded. Private George Townsend, who had ridden behind Griff, was killed. The first company fatality by Indian hands. By the time the Indians retreated and the other men were able to go out and retrieve Townsend's body, the corpse was so badly scalped and mutilated that it was unrecognizable.

Immediately, the Colonel appeared to abandon his early lofty ideas for peace. He set off with a handful of men and horses 20 miles in pursuit. The only thing they returned with when they came back the next day was severe frostbite. "On and after today," Colonel Dimon announced to the assembled regiment, "all armed Indians except those dressed in soldier uniforms and those on the west side of the Missouri River will be regarded as enemies and will be immediately fired upon, and, if possible, killed."

The men seemed eager to follow the order, especially those who had seen Townsend when he was brought back into the fort.

Cold tightened its strangle hold. The fort was guarded

every hour, day and night, by lonely, freezing sentinels who watched from the blockhouse in four-hour shifts. When Griff's turn to do guard duty came, the mercury registered −22°. Griff felt so cold and miserable that he thought he might die. He walked and marched and kept moving to keep warm.

"Sit down, will you? You're making me nervous," said Wallace, who was also on guard duty. He leaned against the wall and stared into the bleak, white distance. "What's that?"

"What?" Griff demanded.

"Don't you see it? Down there by the east side of the river. Looks like someone with a rifle. It's an Indian. I'm sure of it. Look at the way she's walking. She's pointing something this way."

Wallace took aim. He licked his lips nervously.

Griff peered into the distance. "Stop!" he grabbed Wallace's rifle.

"What you doing, fool?" Wallace demanded. "That's an Indian. Colonel said shoot all Indians."

Griff didn't stop to explain. He propped his rifle against the wall and ran as fast as he could down the block-house ladder. He crept through the gate and ran through the snow toward the shape. "Alma!" he shouted. "What do you think you're doing?"

Alma looked up, surprised. She held in her hand the spear and hoop. "Playing."

"Don't you know," Griff said breathlessly, "you aren't

supposed to leave the fort? Nearly got yourself killed. Maybe get me killed too." He glanced up at the other sentinels. Quickly, he scooped her up under one arm and hauled her back up the hill. As he ran, he waved and shouted, "Don't shoot! Don't shoot!"

Alma kicked Griff hard when he placed her back on her own two feet inside the fort. But Griff did not care. He took her by her arm and steered her across the parade grounds to her father's store. "Your daughter, Major," he said.

Major Galpin looked down at Alma with a pale expression. "Where were you? We were worried to death."

"By the river," she said simply.

"She nearly was killed, sir. Pickets thought she was . . . an enemy." Griff wiped his sweating face with his sleeve. His nose was running badly, and he was overheated in the small, hot room.

"Is this true?" Major Galpin demanded.

Alma nodded reluctantly. "I am lonely and bored. Nobody will play."

"Cheewink," Major Galpin said in a slow, sad voice. "Go to your mother now. I will speak to you later."

Griff watched, amazed. He had expected her father to punish her. Pa would have beaten him black-and-blue. Yet nothing happened to Alma. Only a reprimand.

Major Galpin looked very old as he took out his pipe and filled it with tobacco. He was a tall, gray-haired man who had spent most of his life on the Upper Missouri in the fur-trade business. "Take anything from the store you want," Major Galpin said in a low voice.

"What for, sir?" Griff asked.

"Your reward. You saved my daughter's life."

Griff could hardly believe his good fortune. Major Galpin's store shelves were packed with blankets and pails and buckets and shovels. He had tobacco and all kinds of wonderful warm clothing. Griff was fingering a fine wool coat when he was suddenly aware of someone watching him from the corner of the store.

Louisa.

Griff cleared his throat. He felt his face flush. He remembered what she had said about good works and going to heaven. "I don't want anything," he said quietly.

"Nothing?" Major Galpin replied in disbelief.

"No, sir. I was glad to save your daughter. Don't need no reward." He turned and quickly left the store.

The cold hit him in full force and brought him back to his senses. He felt like a fool. There were so many things he needed. So many things he could use when he made his escape. He couldn't believe how stupid he had been to refuse Major Galpin's offer. And for what? To impress a girl who was too old, too cruel, and too beautiful to notice him.

Day's passed. As food rations shrank and the men became too afraid to go hunting far for fresh game, scurvy took its toll. Even Wiley, who was normally the most robust of any, complained that his bones ached and his teeth hurt and he felt terribly tired all the time.

Late in January, the month Alma called the Moon of the Popping Trees, Wiley was confined to the hospital. The hospital grew more and more crowded with each passing day. And good food was harder and harder to come by. Griff was disgusted when he found out about Wiley's honesty. Didn't Wiley notice that the only soldiers who got enough to eat were the ones who bribed the cooks? The best food from the company kitchen was being used to buy favors from the squaws who lived in tepees outside the fort. Griff decided something had to be done. He carefully removed money from his secret hiding place in the barracks. He paid the cooks five dollars to get a decent bowl of soup with more than a shred of vegetable and a bit of meat in it. Then he carried the steaming bowl to the hospital to Wiley, who sat up in bed looking weak and miserable.

"Look what I've got for you," Griff said, surprised at how glad he was to see Wiley again. "Ain't too warm, but it's still good. Taste it."

Wiley smiled and seemed delighted by the visit and the treat. He ate the soup eagerly. "You're a fine person, Griff. A genuine human being," Wiley said. He wiped the corner of his eye with his sleeve.

Griff quickly said goodbye and made his escape out of the hospital. He did not believe one word that Wiley had said.

Griff hurried past a group shoveling out a new

outhouse. In spite of the cold weather and threatening blizzards, Colonel Dimon had kept them all busy. He organized classes in tactics and army regulations.

What was more intrusive, however, were Colonel Dimon's orders regarding cleanliness. He ordered that barracks floors were to be washed every other week. Any soldier appearing on duty with dirty face or hands was fined. He even told company commanders that they were held responsible for every man in their company washing themselves thoroughly once a week.

Once a week! Griff had never washed himself once a week his whole life, and he wasn't about to start now.

Griff shook off the snow from his coat and stood beside the small stove inside the barracks. "What are you doing?" he asked Wallace, who was bent over a desk.

"Writing," Wallace replied. He bit the tip of his pen and gazed off into space.

Griff wandered closer. Ever since the severe weather had set in, some of the boys had started a newspaper. They called it The *Frontier Scout*. Griff couldn't read a word, but he still liked to hear the jokes read aloud, especially when they were funny. "You writing something for the paper?" Griff asked.

"As a matter of fact, I'm writing a poem."

"For the newspaper?"

"For a lady. I'm mailing it home with the next mail."

Griff craned his neck in a casual way. He did not wish to appear too interested. The thing that Wallace was writing did not look like the letter that Louisa had written for him. The poem had only a few scribbles on each line. "Do ladies like such things?" Griff asked.

Wallace nodded solemnly. "The surest way to a woman's heart is a sonnet."

"I thought you said you was writing a poem."

Wallace sighed. "A sonnet is a poem, my good fellow. Now will you leave me in peace? I am trying to compose."

"I know a surefire up-country love charm," Griff bragged. "Take seven hairs from a blood snake, seven scales from a rattlesnake, seven bits of feather from an owl, add a hair from the person you desire, a bit of nail paring, and cook these seven minutes over a hot fire with first rainwater caught in April. Sprinkle this concoction on the clothes of the person you're trying to charm. It won't fail."

Wallace laughed derisively. "That's the most ridiculous thing I've ever heard. Poetry is the way to a woman's heart, not mumbo jumbo up-country charms."

Humiliated, Griff studied his feet. As he did, he noticed a paper crumpled up on the floor. While Wallace was busy scribbling again, Griff picked up the paper. He strolled casually down to the end of the barracks. In one of the corners, he took the paper from his pocket and spread it out and flattened it with his hand. It looked exactly like one of the poems that Wallace was working on. Griff had an idea. He knew exactly what he'd do with this paper. But first he'd have to make it presentable.

He smoothed it and flattened it by placing it under his

mattress. He tried sitting on the paper. Eventually most of the creases disappeared. Then he folded it the same way he'd seen Louisa fold his letter. Silently, he hurried outside the barracks. The wind blew. Snow flew in his face. "Shut that door!" one of his bunkmates shouted.

Griff turned up his collar and hurried across the parade grounds. The snow was falling fast now. *The way to a woman's heart*, he told himself over and over for courage. Finally, he arrived at Alma and Louisa's door. He called, "Anyone home?"

"Who wants to know?" Major Galpin's voice boomed above the wind.

Griff suddenly felt as if he might vomit. He had not counted on Major Galpin pulling aside the tent flap. "I have something here, sir," Griff said weakly. He could not turn back now. Yet he could not think of a handy excuse why he was standing outside their tent in the middle of a blizzard.

A hand thrust out between the tent flaps. It was Major Galpin's hand. "Give it to me. Who's it for?"

"Louisa," Griff said before he could stop himself. Quickly, he placed the paper inside Major Galpin's hand.

"Better get back under cover. This is going to be a very bad storm. Men have been known to be lost while talking to each other in this kind of Dakota blizzard," Major Galpin warned. The tent flap was quickly secured.

Griff felt a tremendous sense of relief as he hurried back to the barracks. He could hardly wait to hear what

Louisa would think of the spectacular poem he had delivered.

However, by the next day, Griff soon found out the awful truth. Everyone in the fort thought it terribly funny that Louisa had somehow become the owner of a complete list of Wallace's laundry, including his underwear.

Next time, Griff decided, he'd stick to mumbo jumbo up-country charms.

For two solid days, the winds raged and the snow fell. The blizzard boomed and howled and threatened to tear the roof off the barracks. Griff cowered in his bed with all his clothes on. He and the others shared what little hard tack they had and melted snow on the small stove for drinking water. Some men played cards. Others prayed. There were no windows in the barracks, so neither Griff nor any of the other men knew just how much snow had fallen. Griff could hardly sleep he felt so cold, so forlorn. What if they were buried alive? He tried to imagine his future riches to keep his mind off the idea that he might never see the light of day again.

Finally, the wind stopped. "We're saved," Wallace said. He found a stick and poked it through the spaces in between the logs in the ceiling. "It's deeper than I thought," he said nervously.

When the men opened the door, they were confronted with a solid wall of white. Frantically, they began to dig their way out with their hands, plates, anything they could find. It took hours to burrow a tunnel to freedom. But when they finally broke through the 10 feet of drifted snow, they were amazed at what they saw. "Come look, Griff!" Wallace shouted. He poked his head up through the snow tunnel opening.

Griff crept up the tunnel on his hands and knees and looked out on a level sea of white. All familiar landmarks were gone. Drifts had been shaped into eerie forms by the wind. Nothing in the fort looked the way he remembered. And over them all, the sun shone with a blinding fierceness. The cold sucked away their breath and made their nostrils freeze shut. Even their words seemed to hang in the air. Smoke from their crooked tin smokestack did not float up. It floated sideways. This was a strange, terrifying world. In less than two days, Griff knew they would have eaten their last bit of food. How would any wagons or sleighs get through these mountains of snow? If there were any animals out there, they must have all perished in the blizzard.

Griff's stomach growled. And for the first time, he wondered if he would have been better off staying in Point Lookout. He might have been hungry there too, but at least he was never in danger of being frozen, lost, buried alive, starved to death, or killed and mutilated by Indians.

Chapter 9

In late March, just when Griff thought he couldn't stand the prison of cold and white bleakness any longer, the wind suddenly shifted from the south. The sun shone, and the air became soft and chanted across the land. Snow melted. Drifts shrank. The barracks' roof dripped constant, muddy rivulets that overflowed the buckets that the men had placed on the floor.

Griff felt restless. He saw Louisa's face in the water buckets, in the knots in the cottonwood log walls. Her voice invaded his dreams and made him miserable. He tried not to think of her. His only hope loomed with the coming of spring and the breakup of ice on the river. Soon he would set himself free and escape the fort forever.

Wild geese sensed the change in season too. Every day a new long line of dark, raucous calling flying north filled the sky. Mrs. Larned, who knew about such things, told

Griff that the wild geese were a sure sign of spring on its way. Some of the other soldiers weren't impressed. They got drunk and shot at the birds.

Strange noises emerged from the frozen Missouri. The ice shivered and boomed. Whenever the weather turned foggy and mild, the river groaned all night long and kept Griff awake. During the day the ice snapped and cracked, and finally fissures appeared. Black water oozed and bubbled up. Griff watched, amazed. He felt as if he were watching a yawning giant finally awaken. The river shouted, shook itself, and roared in white-lipped torrents. The current shoved whole trees; it tumbled and smashed great blocks of ice. Even though the Missouri was still too treacherous for steamboat travel, Griff found an excuse every day to look down river for a sign of a belching smokestack.

On this particular mild morning, Griff had been given a special errand. He was to deliver a message to the Cardwells' tent. He had never visited their tent and felt a bit shy as he knocked on the wooden board that served to brace the canvas.

"Come in, please," a honey-sweet Southern voice said. The familiarity of the woman's accent made Griff think of home. He didn't want to. It just happened automatically, like blinking. He smelled wood smoke, and he remembered his gnawing hunger on the Carolina farm where there was never enough to eat and no one ever spoke his name except to shout some order or hurl some harm.

Carefully, he parted the tent flap and stepped inside. He was amazed to see how crowded the tent was. Every chair, every cot was occupied by a female. They all studied him. His immediate reaction was to flee.

"Now don't go, sir," Mrs. Cardwell said and smiled. Her warm, kind glance immobilized him. "What's your name? I don't recognize you."

"Name's Griff, ma'am," he mumbled. He slipped off his grubby cap and twisted it in his hand. The others were smiling at him too. He blushed and handed Mrs. Cardwell the envelope from the captain.

"He's from Carolina," Alma said in a bright voice. She jumped up and leapt to his side to hold his hand. "He's my friend."

The women laughed. Griff felt his face burning with embarrassment. He would have shaken off her sticky, sweaty grip but he couldn't. He felt too paralyzed.

"Please sit down, sir," Mrs. Cardwell said. She motioned to a chair beside Louisa, who was knitting something. Mrs. Cardwell rose with some difficulty and filled a cup of tea at the little stove.

Alma led Griff to the cot. She sat down next to him and let go of his hand. He could smell her hair, and it smelled greasy. On the other side of him was Louisa. He refused to look at her or to acknowledge her presence. All he wanted to do was to get out of the airless, crowded tent filled with these alien creatures. He stared at his dirty fingernails.

"Here you go, sir," Mrs. Cardwell said. "Sorry we

haven't any sugar." She moved slowly back to her chair.

"Thank you, ma'am," Griff replied. He held the hot tin cup gingerly in his hand. When he took a sip, the tea burned his lip but he tried not to act as if it were painful. He glanced at Mrs. Cardwell and was surprised to see how fat she'd grown since he'd last seen her on their march north. He wondered if it was another strange fashion. Women were always puffing themselves out in odd, hideous ways.

"Griff's one of my bakery's best customers," Mrs. Larned said. "I suppose he's grown at least four inches since fall." She held up the ridiculously tiny sock she was knitting. "Can you imagine that once upon a time your mama made a little bootee this tiny for you?"

Alma and the women laughed again.

Griff felt as if he were shrinking. *Why do they plague me like this?* Secretly, he began to wonder if all women were so untrustworthy. One minute offering tea, the next minute, insults.

"I hear Dr. Herrick's taken sick," Louisa said. She sat very straight on the edge of the cot. Griff wondered if Sister Mary Margaret said she had the best posture at the convent too.

"I don't even like to think of what will become of us if he is called to meet his Maker," Mrs. Larned said, shaking her head sadly. "So much scurvy. Every day the cemetery looks more and more civilized. Nearly eighty grave markers. Can you believe it? And when William and I came, there was only one."

No one spoke for several moments.

Mrs. Cardwell gave a polite cough as if to signal a change in subject. "And so, Griff," she said in a bright voice, "I would think that a fine young man like yourself would be performing in our new upcoming theatrical. What part do you have in Colonel Dimon's newest extravaganza?"

Griff cleared his throat. "None, ma'am." He had purposefully avoided the makeshift theater that Colonel Dimon had created to "raise morale." The shoulder-straps thought it amusing to dress up in gauze beards and wave their arms around and sing Northern patriotic songs. Not Griff.

"You really must participate," Louisa said. She leaned toward him ever so slightly. "I do not have much of a singing voice myself, but I have found performing to be very wholesome and enjoyable."

"You sing very well, Louisa," Eagle Woman spoke up. She sat in the corner where she seemed to be carefully stitching a patch on a worn gingham dress.

Louisa forced a smile, but she did not look at her mother. "When Alma goes to the convent this fall to start school, she, too, will learn to sing."

"I am not going," Alma announced. "I am going to Grandmother."

"*Mi cunk she,*" Eagle Woman said in a soft voice, "I know you miss our people, but you cannot go to their village. It is too dangerous."

"I am not afraid," Alma said stubbornly. She stood up and knocked over Griff's tea.

"Always making a mess! You are such a nuisance,"

95

Louisa exclaimed. Her voice sounded very loud in the small, crowded tent.

"It's nothing. I can clean it," Griff mumbled. His ears rang as he wiped up the spot on the cot with his hat.

"You come back here," Louisa demanded. "Mother, make her come back here."

Eagle Woman said nothing as Alma darted out the door. The tent door flapped. A fresh warm breeze drifted inside. The other women did not speak.

Griff decided that this was his chance to escape too. "Well, I thank you kindly for the tea. I must be going," Griff said. He stood up carefully, terrified he might also knock something over. How did these women manage to sit in this small, confined space and still manage to breathe? He wondered if they had huddled in overheated tents like this one all winter. Perhaps that was why he seldom saw many of them about.

Suddenly, like the unexpected arrival of the warm spring wind, Louisa's attitude changed. She gently placed her hand on his arm and said in a beguiling voice, "I hope to see you at the rehearsal this evening."

Griff mumbled something incoherent and backed out of the tent, still twisting his tea-soaked cap. When he stepped outdoors into the bright light, he did not even think of looking for Alma. All he could think about was the soft pressure on his arm and the look in Louisa's dark eyes. Even though she was part Indian, he decided, she was still the most beautiful creature he had ever seen.

That evening Griff combed his hair and washed his

face and hands and put on his only clean shirt.

"Where you going?" Wiley demanded.

"To the rehearsal," Griff said. He tried very hard to sound somewhat bored by the idea.

As soon as he left the barracks, he hurried across the parade grounds to make sure he wasn't late. The officers' barracks was the only housing with a real wooden floor. There were walls with shelves, and tables with chairs that had backs—not just hard benches. While the privates ate fried salt pork and dried peas, the officers dined on oyster pie and pickled herring at Christmas. That was what Wallace told him. Naturally, Griff was curious if some delicacy like strawberries or sponge cake might be served in the officers' quarters this evening. That would at least make going to this rehearsal worthwhile.

As soon as he came into the well-lit room, he was greeted warmly by Mrs. Larned, who gave him a confidential wink. He felt worse than ever. Then he heard Louisa's charming laughter. She was surrounded by a great flock of officers wearing coats with gleaming buttons. They all must have known she was part Indian, yet obviously none of them cared. When she smiled at them, her teeth shimmered. She did not bother to look at Griff.

Captain Fay thrust a sheet into his hands. "Good man. Here are the words to the song we're practicing."

Griff's stomach turned. He held the page and stared at the undecipherable scratches. What did they say? He felt too humiliated to ask.

"All right. Let's begin. You fellows stand over here.

Miss Louisa and Mrs. Larned, you two on this side. What's your name?"

"Private Allen, sir," Griff mumbled.

"Private Allen, you're over here."

Mrs. Cardwell, who perched on a chair, blew a few notes into a silver flute. Everyone hummed. Everyone except Griff. His hands were sweating so much that his song page went limp. In his whole life, he'd been to the Baptist church back home only twice. And when it came time to sing a hymn, he simply mouthed the words.

The booming voices around him rang out so loudly that they hurt Griff's ears. His head throbbed. Louisa and the other officers seemed to actually know how to make musical words come out of their mouths. And what was even more amazing, they seemed to enjoy the experience. Griff watched out of the corner of his eye as Louisa opened her pretty mouth in an O-shape. She sounded exactly like a warbler in the woods. Her eyes shone. The other officers shot her admiring glances and grinned so hard that their faces looked as if they might crack.

"Private Allen?" Captain Fay spoke up. "We aren't getting any support from the alto section."

"Sir?" Griff asked in complete puzzlement.

"I can't understand the words you're singing. Please sing louder."

Griff pursed his dry lips. He felt sweat trickle down the insides of his sleeves. His tongue felt thick and cottony in his mouth.

Suddenly, Louisa's trebling birdlike voice rang out,

"Now Captain Fay, you are going to have to be patient with our newest member of the chorus."

Griff felt a vague sense of relief. Louisa was on his side. She would help him. She was an angel.

"You see, he doesn't know how to read," Louisa said. She put her hand to her mouth in a fetching way and giggled.

All the other officers found Griff's inability to read very funny. They laughed too.

Griff bolted from the chorus. He didn't hear anything, not even Mrs. Larned as she called to him. In an instant, he squashed the song sheet, threw it on the floor, and escaped out the door. Laughter rang in his ears even as he rushed away from the officers' barracks.

"How was the rehearsal?" Wiley asked when Griff returned.

Wretchedly, Griff threw himself on his pallet and covered his face with his blanket. "Worse than Gettysburg," he replied in a muffled voice.

The next day the wind began to howl. The temperature dropped. For three days and nights, blizzards battered the fort. The snow fell so hard and so fast, and the wind blew with such ferocity, that no one dared leave the barracks.

Griff and the other soldiers wearily began to dig out as soon as the storm ended. Drifts piled up in some places nearly 30 feet high. It was the worst blizzard they had experienced so far. "Hard to believe it's April," Wiley grumbled. He and Griff plowed through the deep snow in search of any surviving cattle.

Griff had three scarves wrapped around his face. He fell into snow up to his waist and had to be dug out by Wiley. They struggled along beside one side of the fence. Not a living thing could be seen on the horizon.

Griff pulled the scarf from his mouth. It was damp and sour-smelling from his breath. When he spoke, the air burned his lungs. "I bet every last cow's been frozen to death. How many we counted smothered so far?"

"Twelve," Wiley replied.

Griff looked hopelessly out over the cruel, endless expanse of snow. *Maybe I'll never escape.*

Chapter 10

Up-country folks back in South Carolina used to say, "Never trouble trouble 'til trouble troubles you." Some translated that as, "Don't argue with the wind." For Griff, it seemed that Colonel Dimon had a peculiar knack for arguing with the wind and making life worse than it already was for everybody.

The arrogant Yankee officer misinterpreted what Indian chiefs told him. He riled friendly tribes and inflamed hostiles. And of course it was the lowly privates who paid the price for Colonel Dimon's mistakes. Their lives were on the line every time they left the stockade to herd cattle or cut timber.

By mid-April, barely 300 men remained scurvy-free and fit enough to perform their duties. Griff noticed, however, that there seemed to be an endless supply of Indians intent on running off cattle and wiping out what was left of the fort's company. Like Mosby's Raiders back in Virginia, the Indian warriors appeared and vanished without warning. They were skilled riders, crack shots with rifles, and remarkably adept at shooting arrows at full gallop.

On April 12, more than 200 mounted Cheyenne and Sioux from the Platte River country swept down out of the hills near the fort and ambushed herders outside the stockade. The biggest group of attacking Indians yet had painted themselves and their spectacular ponies in wild and terrifying colors. They wore feathers and strips of fur and decorated their spears and shields with scalp-locks. The intimidating sight and sound of so many yowling warriors riding flat-out on ponies was enough to paralyze many of the soldiers.

Two privates were riddled with arrows and died before they made it back inside. Thirty-six cows, 19 mules and 13 horses were run off. Three days later, more than 300 Indians riding magnificent ponies dashed around a group of herders a mile from the fort. Nineteen-year-old Private Hiram Watson from Georgia was hit with an arrow in the chest and never recovered.

Griff, who miraculously remained healthy, found himself on duty nearly round the clock. One afternoon he stood guard in the warm sunshine atop the blockhouse. He leaned against the wall and looked out over the plains. For the past week, temperatures had soared. Snow drifts shrank. The wind felt gentle against his face. In the distance he heard the incessant clatter of sandhill cranes. Flies buzzed. It was dry in the blockhouse, unlike the soggy barracks or the fort's muddy parade grounds. Griff yawned. So peaceful . . . so quiet . . . so warm. . . .

"Private!"

Griff's eyes flew open. He found himself crouching on the blockhouse floor. He was curled up in a ball with his arms around his gun. A rough hand grabbed him by the back of the collar and yanked him to his feet. "You're under arrest," the lieutenant barked in his ear.

"Arrest?" Griff stammered.

"That's right. You'll be lucky if you aren't court-martialed for sleeping on guard duty. Get moving."

"Where?" Griff said, trembling. He remembered what had happened to Private Dowdy. Colonel Dimon was crazy. What would he do to him?

"Guardhouse," the lieutenant said. He marched Griff to the ladder. They both descended. Then the lieutenant shoved him toward the small, low-roofed building near the magazine, where the gunpowder was stored. The soldiers liked to joke that the guardhouse's location was the colonel's idea. Prisoners would be the first to blow up if the fort ever caught fire.

The lieutenant unbolted and swung open the guardhouse door. Several pale, blinking men hurried toward the light. "Let us out, will you?" Private Francis McCarthy begged. He was an Irishman who had been locked up for mutiny. After punching a corporal, he bragged that he could whip any man who thought an Irishman wouldn't fight.

"We can hardly breathe. Will you look at this roof? It's dripping like a sieve," declared Private J. R. Lucky. He was serving time for refusing to beat a drum. "And we ain't got proper blankets. Tell Surgeon Herrick. We'll soon be sick as dogs."

"Smells like dogs in here too," the lieutenant said. He reminded Griff of Beadle, the guard at Point Lookout. They both had the same glinty evil eyes when they smiled. "You fellows should have thought a bit harder before you disobeyed Colonel's rules." He slammed the door shut.

"Strutting Yankee tyrant," McCarthy hissed. "Hope you die with your throat cut and your tongue stretched on some savage's trophy stick."

Somebody chuckled on the other side of the cottonwood log wall.

"Who's in there?" Griff asked, jerking his thumb toward the other guardhouse room.

"Two Santee prisoners from Minnesota. The Colonel's shooting them tomorrow," Lucky replied in a matter-of-fact voice.

"What for?" Griff said nervously.

Lucky shrugged his shoulders. "Maybe he don't like their faces."

"Maybe for revenge for Watson and the others who got killed," McCarthy said. He took a pack of cards from his pocket and squatted on the ground. Expertly, he shuffled the deck.

Griff peered between the cracks of the cottonwood logs and saw two middle-aged Indians with blankets around their shoulders. They sat in a pile of dirty hay. They stared straight ahead and did not speak. Their faces revealed no emotion. Griff wondered if they knew he was watching them.

"Want to play?" McCarthy said.

In the thin light that entered between the unchinked logs, Griff surveyed his seven fellow prisoners in a room that was no bigger than a chicken coop. He made up his mind. When he had his first opportunity, he was running away on the first steamboat north.

Time crawled. Griff couldn't remember what day it was. He checked the guardhouse room next door and saw that the Indians were gone.

"Hey, Griff? You in there?"

Excitedly, Griff peered out through the logs. Good old Wiley. "You all right?" Wiley demanded. He was holding something in his hand. "Brought you some food."

The other prisoners immediately looked up. They were all hungry.

"Just a moment, Wiley," Griff said cautiously then turned to the other prisoners with a smile. "Here's the deal. I provide you fellows with news. In return, I get the food. Agreed?"

They nodded and licked their lips.

"So Wiley, tell us what's happening out there," Griff said.

Wiley took a moment to peer over his shoulder. "Ice is

clear on the river. They're expecting the *Yellowstone* to be the first steamboat to come through any day."

The other prisoners cheered.

"What else?" Griff demanded.

Wiley lowered his voice and stepped closer. "I heard they're going to give you eighteen months hard labor and maybe forfeit your pay."

Griff's shoulders sagged. *Eighteen months!* He wouldn't stay in this place eighteen more hours if he could help it.

"What about Francis McCarthy?" McCarthy demanded.

"Two months hard labor," Wiley replied. "Lucky got two months too. Adams? You got four months hard labor. Same for Johnson, Snead, Roach, and Thompson."

Everyone seemed relieved they would not be executed.

"And something else," Wiley said, his voice barely a whisper.

"What?" Griff said.

"Wallace's run off. He's gone upriver. That's what the boys say. Two others went with them. Everybody thinks they stole an Indian's bull boat."

Griff felt stunned. He couldn't breathe. This was the worst news of all. Wallace was gone to the gold fields. He'd left without him.

"They'll be lucky they make it a mile without losing their scalps," McCarthy said and spit. The other prisoners murmured in agreement.

Griff cleared his throat. "That was a heap of news.

Thanks, Wiley. You can hand over the grub. Poke it through the widest hole in the wall."

Wiley did as he was told. "Take care of yourself," he said and winked.

Griff tugged the dirty handkerchief. He unwrapped it and found two pieces of bread. He peeked between the slices, hoping for a bit of butter or perhaps a sliver of salt pork. What he found instead was something much more valuable. It was a small, smudged folded piece of paper. When none of the other prisoners was looking, he slipped this inside his pocket.

Later that night, he unfolded the grubby paper and discovered that it was a map. With shaking hands he studied the thick wavy line that he knew must be the Missouri. The other thin wavy lines, he decided, must be smaller streams and rivers. The V-shapes were the Rocky Mountains. And at the very end of the Missouri, where it petered out into a shaky scrawl, were words. He couldn't read them but he already knew what they said because he'd heard the miners speak them with such reverence. *Bannack. Virginia City. Last Chance Gulch. Wind River.*

Griff chewed the last piece of bread slowly and considered Wiley's cleverness in delivering the map. *He wants to escape too.* Why hadn't Griff thought of him before? Wiley was the perfect partner—strong, loyal. He'd never desert Griff like Wallace. Griff made up his mind. Together, he and Wiley would desert and get rich in Montana.

After a week, the prisoners were released. When Griff explained his escape plan to Wiley, the big soldier was delighted. "When do we go?" he whispered.

"Soon as the *Yellowstone* arrives," Griff said. "Don't tell a soul."

For his punishment, Griff was assigned to timber-cutting detail with no time off. The Indians burned the woods across the Missouri. Smoke hung in the air. Griff didn't have to cut any trees for a few days, but that didn't stop him from looking up and down the wild, swirling river for a sign of the steamboat chugging north.

Finally, on May 9, a distant whistle howled louder and louder. A bell clanged. Men raced to the blockhouse for a better view. Smoke curled and belched over the hills. They threw their hats in the air. The *Yellowstone*!

The sight of the great white steamboat was so marvelous, Griff could hardly believe his eyes. Passengers crowded the decks and waved handkerchiefs and hats at the cheering soldiers.

"There she is!" Griff shouted.

"An engine on a raft with $11,000 worth of jigsaw work!" Lucky replied, pointing at the steamboat's intricate woodworking.

Griff knew that he and Wiley wouldn't have much time to sneak aboard and find a place to stow away. He hurried to the barracks amid the confusion of rushing soldiers. He gathered up a small bunch of clothing and supplies, which he had stuffed into a knapsack along with the precious map. Where was Wiley? He searched the crowd along the river's edge but couldn't find him.

"News! News!" someone shouted and waved a newspaper in the air. One of the privates climbed atop a tree stump. A crowd quickly gathered. "Lincoln's been shot!"

Some of the men cheered. Others whistled. A few remained silent as if too stunned to speak.

"Attention!" the lieutenant announced. Scowling, Colonel Dimon marched through the throng with his best dress uniform and shining dress sword swinging at his side. Some of the men backed nervously away from him.

"This is no time for merriment. Anyone found to cheer or revel in this serious time will be taken to the guardhouse and tried as a traitor," Colonel Dimon said and stroked his struggling little moustache. "Proceed and read further. What of the President?" he asked urgently. "Is he dead? Is he—"

"Lee's surrendered," interrupted the soldier on the stump. He slowly lowered the newspaper. He looked pale and did not seem able to read any more.

The crowd murmured in disbelief. Griff rubbed his eyes. Lee would never surrender. Never.

"Well, here is some good news," Colonel Dimon said. "The war must be nearly over. The South's defeated for sure." The officers cheered.

None of the privates joined them. They staggered away, their eyes dull. "Over?" one soldier asked.

"How can it be over?" another answered.

"Come back here, men. Listen to the great and marvelous news!" Colonel Dimon commanded.

Griff shook his head as if trying to emerge from a deep sleep. He had to get moving. He had to think. Where was Wiley?

"Slow down there, man," McCarthy demanded, grabbing Griff by the arm. "You should be glad to hear this. We won't be having to deal with our dear colonel for a few days."

"What do you mean?" Griff asked.

"He's going on the *Yellowstone.* Up to Fort Union or thereabouts. If we're lucky, the ship'll sink and our leader'll be eaten by catfish," McCarthy whispered. "That's good news, it is."

Griff stared at the man, stunned. The colonel was going aboard the *Yellowstone?* His escape plan was ruined. What would happen if he were found hiding aboard the very same ship? "Have you seen Wiley?" he asked, desperate that somehow Wiley had wandered on board.

"No," McCarthy said and scratched his head. "Have you checked the hospital?"

Without bothering to answer, Griff turned away from McCarthy and pushed through the crowd. He ran all the way to sick room. There was Wiley, lying in bed. Wiley tried to smile at Griff. With some effort, he lifted his hand as if to wave him away. "Aren't you supposed to be a-going?" he hissed. "Steamboat's come. I heard the whistle."

"I can't leave you here," Griff answered in a low voice. He glanced up around the room at the other soldiers who were in the rows of beds.

"It's the scurvy plaguing me again," Wiley said. "Collapsed on guard duty. I'll be all right in a while. You go on."

"There'll be other steamboats. Besides, Dimon's taking this one north. We wouldn't get far with him on board. You just get better. I'll wait for you."

Wiley blinked hard. "You're a good man, Griff," he said, barely above a whisper. "A genuine human being."

Griff turned and left before Wiley could see the disappointment on his face.

Chapter 11

Griff could not sleep on this warm May night. The barracks seemed airless. Bedbugs nipped his neck, his face. In the distance came the steady, ominous beating of drums and the piercing chorus of unearthly singing. For the past several days, hundreds of Indians had gathered on the hillsides near Fort Rice. Griff heard that they danced in resplendent feathers and fierce war paint. They sang war songs around huge fires. No one—not even hasty, opinionated Colonel Dimon—seemed to have any idea what the Indians might do next.

During the past 10 days, a half-dozen steamboats had docked and chugged north to take advantage of rising water levels in the river. The crews did not waste a moment as they unloaded supplies at the fort's mooring. Guards and passengers trained their rifle sights on the surrounding bluffs in readiness for Indian ambush. Several steamboats had been attacked, looted, and burned on the way to Fort Benton.

In spite of these dangers, Griff longed to escape upriver. And yet he knew he could not. He had to keep his promise to Wiley. He could not leave without him. But what if Wiley never got better?

On May 24 or thereabouts, Griff had heard a rumor that three steamboats were coming through. That was only a few days away. Would Wiley be well enough to travel by then? Griff had to have a partner—someone dependable who could back him up in a tight place. No one ever got very far upriver alone.

Wallace found that out.

Griff tossed and turned, trying not to think about Wallace's corpse. The day before, the *Deer Lodge* had brought Wallace back for burial after a crew member spotted his blackened, arrow-riddled body floating 20 miles north of the fort. A scrap of First Volunteer uniform knotted around an arrow shaft indicated where Wallace might belong. Whoever killed him had made sure of that.

"Griff, stop your danged jumping about! Can't a fellow get some sleep?" McCarthy demanded in a groggy voice.

"Sorry. Bugs are biting me bad," Griff whispered. The bedbug infestation in the soldiers' straw pallets and in the barracks' log walls was nearly as awful as the hordes of rats and mice that nibbled everything edible—including candles and leather shoes.

"Only way to escape them cursed bedbugs," said

McCarthy, "is to crawl up the fort flagstaff and get a darky to sweep the base round it night and day. That way them critters can't climb up and get you." He chuckled as if he thought himself enormously clever.

"Shut up!" Lucky shouted.

Griff turned over and hoped the 11 potatoes he'd stolen from the *Benton* were safe in the tin box at the foot of his bed. Those potatoes, each no bigger than a baby's fist, were the first he'd seen in nearly a year. He'd cook them up using a special up-country recipe and feed them to Wiley himself if he had to. Those potatoes, he decided, were his last best hope to get Wiley on his feet again.

Griff soon discovered that the potatoes had a miraculous effect on Wiley's health. In three days, Wiley's energy returned. Unfortunately, Captain Fay also noticed his sudden recovery and included Wiley on his logging detail.

"I'll go too," Griff said. He didn't want to let Wiley out of his sight until the next steamboat came through.

"Don't worry none about me," Wiley protested, even though he seemed pleased to have Griff's company.

Griff mounted a bony, swaybacked horse and followed Wiley and a group of three other men plus Captain Fay on horseback. The farther Griff traveled from the fort, the better he felt. In the distance, brittle gray hills had turned faintly green. The sun shone. It seemed like a fine day until Griff glanced on the ground nearby and noticed swarms of young locusts greedily devouring the first green stalks. Their dark, glittering bodies seemed so loathsome that he had to look away.

Ki-raaaaaaa! A hawk screamed overhead.

Suddenly, Griff's horse whinnied. His ears twitched. The other riders' horses must have sensed something too. They pawed the ground.

"You fellows stay here. I'll head up a ways. It's probably nothing." Wiley kicked his horse and trotted ahead. The horse kept its ears straight up.

"We'll back you up," Captain Fay said. "Don't lose sight of us round the bend."

Wiley raised one hand to acknowledge Captain Fay's words. As he did, the underbrush exploded with a dozen or more swift ponies and wildly painted bodies. The warriors' terrifying shrieks made the hair on Griff's neck stand straight up. The Indians plucked steel-tipped arrows from quivers, drew them against their bows, and sent them flying. *Siz-siz-sizzzz.* Slender murderous shafts sliced again and again through the air.

Captain Fay dropped from his horse, aimed his gun, and pulled the trigger. An Indian fell. Griff dismounted. He loaded, fired, and missed. Indians howled derisively. One warrior rode so close to Griff that froth from his pony's red and blue painted flank flecked against Griff's cheek. Griff didn't notice. He fired again. Again he missed. The ravine swarmed with half-naked, yipping, barking, fantastically painted warriors. Their ponies reared and plunged in spangles, colored horsehair, hawk feathers, and

clattering necklaces made from deer hooves. Griff felt
dizzy trying to hit targets swirling around him.

"Go back!" Wiley shouted.

Griff turned in time to see Wiley's horse plunge to its
knees. Wiley flew over the horse's blood-spattered head.
Two Indians raced toward the place where Wiley lay,
crumpled and helpless. Their scalping knives gleamed.

Griff swung into the saddle and dug his heels into his
horse. "Who-ey! Who-ey!" he screamed and charged. He
waved his unloaded gun. The warriors galloped in a wider
circle. They shouted and watched what Griff would do.

Griff jumped from his horse to the ground beside
Wiley, who lay in a pool of blood. Wiley had arrows in his
shoulder, thigh, and back. With strength Griff did not
know he had, he pulled up Wiley's heavy, limp body and
coaxed it partway over his own horse's saddle. He hurried
to the other side and pulled Wiley's arms so that they
hung on the other side. Wiley groaned.

Good. Still alive.

Griff slapped the horse on the flanks. "Go on!" The
horse took off toward the fort with Wiley bouncing and
flopping on his back.

Sweat poured off Griff's forehead into his eyes. He
blinked. And in that instant, he was enveloped in a cloud
of dust kicked up by horse hooves. He loaded, aimed,
fired. A warrior catapulted to the ground. The wounded
Indian was quickly retrieved by another warrior on a pony.

"Fall back! Fall back!" Captain Fay cried. The other

soldiers were already retreating. Bullets pattered against the earth.

In the distance, Griff heard the crash of the howitzer. He knew that the men in the fort must have heard their shots and been alerted to the ambush. A few of the Indians retreated as soon as the first shells fell and exploded. Several others spurred their ponies and circled Griff and the other straggling soldiers on foot. The Indians stretched out flat on their ponies or clung to the far side of them. More shells rocked the air. *Boom-boom-boom.*

Griff dashed on foot toward the fort. He wove in and out, faster than he ever had in his life. The fort gate swung open. Captain Fay and the others escaped to safety inside. Griff was about to enter too, when he spotted his horse plunging through the brush. The rawhide saddle was bloody and empty. The horse snorted with fright. Its tail and mane floated, and its reins flew free. *Where's Wiley?*

"Come on! Get in here while you can!" a soldier called to Griff from the blockhouse.

Griff, now out of ammunition, helplessly scanned the slope near the fort one last time. He spied a blue heap—maybe only 20 yards from the stockade. A warrior in the distance must have spotted it too. The Indian roared with a blood-curdling bellow. He lifted his knife over his head and urged his pony toward the fallen body.

At that very moment, a woman's cry. A blur of movement. Someone running from the fort. Griff watched, horrified. The warrior galloped closer, closer.

Eagle Woman darted, slid. Dust flew. She cradled Wiley's bloody head in her lap just as the pony's hooves nearly trampled her. She rose on her knees. The pony reared. She gestured with her hands and shouted in defiance.

The warrior glared down at her. And in that instant, he turned, circled, and vanished.

For a moment, Griff was certain his heart had stopped beating. His knees shook as he stumbled toward Eagle Woman and Wiley. Two more soldiers rushed from the fort with a makeshift stretcher. Together, they loaded Wiley. His blue eyes fluttered open then shut as he was carried away.

Griff turned to Eagle Woman. The front of her dress, her arms, her face were smeared with blood. Dryness parched Griff's mouth. He could barely speak above a croak. "Ma'am, what did you say to scare him off like that?"

Eagle Woman sighed. "I say, 'This man belongs to me now! You cannot mutilate or touch him.' "

"He could have killed you."

Eagle Woman shrugged as if the remarkably brave thing she had done were nothing.

Wiley lived long enough to look one last time upon Eagle Woman's face. He thanked her and died holding her hand.

On the second day of June, Wiley was buried with full honors. The entire fort had assumed a somber, sorrowful atmosphere that overcast afternoon. Almost everyone wore black armbands. The flag flew at half-mast. Even though these signs of official mourning were for President Lincoln's death, Griff preferred to believe they were for Wiley. Throughout the ceremony, Griff stood straight and tall. He held his mouth tight against the trembling. His eyes glazed. He tried very hard not to feel anything.

That night, high winds kicked up the dust. Lightning shimmered. Thunder crashed. Griff slept fitfully. His dreams drifted him back to Gettysburg and filled his head with smoke and the stink of death and the high, piercing whine of artillery, and the terrible screams for help. . . .

He sat up, determined not to sleep. He'd concentrate on something else. Something pleasant. His future riches.

But even this favorite fantasy did not distract him. Somehow Wiley's stupid grinning face kept creeping into Griff's mind. He imagined Wiley humming irritating tuneless songs the time the South Carolina Volunteers had marched knee-deep in mud as thick as cornmeal batter. He recalled the unnatural way that Wiley never complained during the entire week that they scarcely drew a quarter-pound of flour to each man. They were so hungry that they ate horse feed mixed with salt and a bit of water.

Griff had never in his life known anyone so mulish gullible as Wiley. His childlike, open face gave away every hand of poker he ever had. He was so believing that he never figured out it wasn't Yanks but Griff and the other fellows who played a mean trick and tied all his clothes in tight knots while he was swimming.

Griff sighed. In the darkness he felt very hollow, very empty, very alone. Wiley had been his hope and his dependence. Now he was gone. What would Griff do without him? True, Griff had never dared confide in Wiley all the sadness of his own heart when he was in trouble. He knew that Wiley talked too freely, too generously—the same way he slurped his food so it dribbled down his chin. Even so, Griff missed him. Wiley had given Griff an odd sense of consolation that perhaps everything would work out after all.

Now Griff wasn't so sure.

It was several days later that Griff finally was able to go through Wiley's few possessions. The captain said he intended to send them back to Wiley's family in South Carolina once Griff sorted through what remained. There wasn't much: a dress belt, never worn; one shirt, badly patched; and a wooden box whittled with a crude picture of a woman. Inside the box was the bell Griff had given him. It was still tied with a grubby loop of string. Griff pocketed the bell. He looked inside Wiley's wallet and found a practically worthless Confederate dollar, a lock of hair, and a newspaper clipping. He stared at the words and wondered what inspired Wiley to save them.

He did not want the other fellows to make fun of Wiley's memory, in case the words said something silly. So he decided to go to Louisa. Perhaps it would help her go to Heaven if she assisted Griff by deciphering the clipping.

It took Griff nearly three hours to get up the courage to go to Louisa's tent. "Can you read this for me, ma'am?" he asked as politely as he could. He did not dare look into her eyes. He sensed for the first time that there was something about her that charmed him the same way the dazzling, brilliant eyes of the rattlesnake transfixed small animals. He wouldn't be tricked this time. He'd remain strong.

Louisa took the newspaper clipping. She cleared her throat and read aloud:

> "If I die far from thee, my love
> Oh bury me between a turtle dove
> To show to your dearest love
> In years to come I died for love."

"That's it?" Griff shook his head in disgust. It seemed like a ridiculous thing to bother carrying around all this time. Just as he was about to retrieve the ragged, yellow paper, he noticed something strange.

Louisa was crying. "It's . . . it's so beautiful," she said between sobs.

Baffled by her tears, Griff did not know what to say. He did not know what to do.

" 'I died for love.' " She removed an impeccably white handkerchief and dabbed her eyes. "Oh, I can barely look at that line again. Where did you get this poem?"

Griff coughed. He tried not to look at her. He felt too

embarrassed. "I found it in Wiley's wallet after he died."

Hearing this, Louisa burst into fresh sobs.

"I'm sorry if it makes you so sad, ma'am. Wouldn't have brung it to you if I knew it would break you up so bad," Griff said. He wanted nothing more than to hightail it out of sight.

"The words make me sad," Louisa insisted, "because they're so beautiful."

"Beautiful?" Griff said in wonderment. "More like ridiculous if you ask me. Don't make no sense. Who would die for love? I wouldn't."

Louisa looked up at him. Her dark eyes, which seconds earlier had been swimming in tears, now flashed with anger. "I wouldn't expect someone like you to understand," she said coldly. "You may go."

Griff awkwardly retreated. He would never understand women. Never.

On his way back to the barracks, Griff picked up two hefty chunks of mud. For no good reason he hurled them against the side of Colonel Dimon's cabin as hard as he could. *Thud! Thud!*

"Who's there?" someone shouted.

Griff hurried away, strangely satisfied.

Chapter 12

Summer roared with a ferocious rush into the country. Grass grew thick and green; cottonwoods and willows leafed out double-quick. Mosquitoes and every kind of flying, biting bug abounded. It seemed to Griff that as soon as the long white frozen sleep ended, the plains were thrown into wild green abandon to make up for lost time. Even the heat was stronger, more potent than the kind he'd remembered back home. Sometimes the air felt thick and heavy. Any kind of work drenched a fellow in sweat that never cooled him.

Then without warning, low in the west, a dark wall of bruised clouds might appear. In minutes a sudden cool black curtain drew across the landscape. Earsplitting thunder smacked. Heavy drops cratered the dust. A windswept sheet of water slashed and bent anything standing—be it grass or tree or flagpole. Just as suddenly as the storm came, it vanished. The sky brightened from dark gray to pearl to pale blue again. The sun blazed and made everything wet glitter and shimmer.

Throughout June, steamboat whistles echoed up and down the river. Soldiers at Fort Rice enthusiastically greeted the arrival of the *David Watts*, the *St. John*, the *Silver Lake*, the *Hattie May*, and the *Cutter*. Some boats hurried north. Others floated south, laden with miners and thousands of dollars worth of gold dust. More than a few carried grim news: the *Cutter* and the *St. John* lost crew members in a fierce attack upriver with Indians. One river pilot narrowly missed a direct shot to his forehead.

Griff heard the rumors of a big Indian attack and watched the comings and goings of boats with a growing sense of confusion and anxiety. He knew he had to leave before the river level began to drop. He had to go alone. There was no other way.

Secretly, he gathered and hid what he needed. A piece of rope. Extra food. At Major Galpin's store, he had seen a tin box of sulphur-tipped matches. The matches would come in handy because he could build a fire quickly with them. A fire would keep him warm, cook his food— maybe even save his life. Yes, he needed the matches. But how could he get them? He had spent all his money.

Alma. She would get them for him.

On a particularly sunny afternoon after an unusually peaceful week, Griff found Alma sitting beside her family's tent. She poked the ground with a stick. "What're you doing?" he asked.

"Nothing," she replied and made a sad face.

"Want to help me? I told Dr. Herrick I'd gather up some compass plant. Says it's good for coughs and fevers. Don't know what compass plant looks like, do you?"

She nodded. "Much compass plant up on Wagon Wheel Bluff. I'll take you."

"That's pretty far away."

"You promise to go with me, remember? You scared?" Alma demanded derisively.

Griff shook his head and thought of Alma's mother and her fierce bravery. He felt a little weak and foolish. "I'll bring my gun," he said in a brusque voice.

The way up to Wagon Wheel Bluff was along a dry dusty trail. The trail followed a ridge around a pile of rocks. Barefoot, Alma nimbly scrambled up while Griff struggled, out of breath, behind her. When they reached the top, Griff could see the crooked, treacherous Missouri far below. In the distance were the faint traces of the barren hills and chalky bluffs of the Badlands, a place General Sully had named "hell with the fires burned out."

Griff looked around the bluff and saw that scrap iron in twisted shapes littered the ground. Weeds grew up between the spokes of weathered wagon wheels. A snake slithered around a rusty tin can. Debris lay scattered: ax handles, broken china dishes, part of a coffee mill, a bent spoon, a grindstone, a shredded scrap of blanket. Griff kicked an empty warped picture frame and wished he had a piece of bone from a boiled black cat to keep away haunts. "What is this place?"

"Sam say this is where the Santee came with wagons, horses, supplies," Alma said in a matter-of-fact voice. She picked up a rusted latch that looked as if it had once been part of a trunk. She poked a pile of rotten wood.

"What were the Santee doing?"

"Running away," Alma said and sighed. "After the big fight in Minnesota, they have to get away from the soldiers. They take wagons and supplies with them but only get this far. Soldiers chase them. So the Santee burn and push over a cliff many wagons. Then they try to escape up river."

Griff imagined battalions of blue-coated soldiers struggling over the plains. He had heard about the fight. They called it the Minnesota Massacre. He'd never considered what went on after the fighting and the burning of the white settlements had ended. "What happened to the Indians?"

"Some escape. Some hung by neck. Some killed by other Indians."

Alma's matter-of-fact voice gave Griff pause. It felt odd to be sitting here discussing a massacre with someone who was part Indian. There was, of course, nothing terrifying about Alma. She did not seem to have anything to do with the other soldiers' wild Indian scalping stories. She was just a little girl sitting on a broken wagon tongue.

Alma rubbed her forehead and squinted as if she wanted to talk about something else. "Sorry to hear about your friend who went up the spout."

Griff sat down too. He tossed a rusty nail in the air. "You mean Wiley?"

Alma nodded. "My mother say he call your name when he's dying."

Griff turned away so she could not see his face.

"You not know?"

Griff shook his head. He was afraid to speak, afraid that the sadness and bitter loneliness clogging his throat would creep up out of his mouth and make him seem foolish and weak. Someone to be pitied. He didn't want that. So he said nothing.

"He's not gone away from you forever. Grandmother says all beings at death leave their bodies and travel on the Spirit Trail in the sky to the Land of Many Lodges. You see that place in sky at night. Pa calls it the Milky Way."

Griff sighed. He wished he could believe in something. Alma's words were a kind of comfort, but he did not trust them. Her words were Indian words.

Alma jumped to her feet. "Look!" She tugged at a long-stemmed plant with tough roots.

"Is this what Dr. Herrick wants?" He tugged too. The big leaves were nearly a foot long.

"Some Indians won't camp near too much compass plant. Say lightning strike." She smiled slyly at Griff. "Watch out!" She whacked him with a bunch of fat stems.

He yelped and chased her around and around the wagon tongue. She laughed and laughed. Out of breath, she sat down. Griff stood with his hands in his pockets.

Something jingled. He pulled out Wiley's bell.

"What's that?" She studied the dangling, singing silver object. Her eyes gleamed like a fascinated crow.

Griff chuckled. Suddenly, he felt inspired. "Want to trade?"

Alma nodded eagerly.

"A box of sulphur-tipped matches, an ax, and a bag of cornmeal from your father's store."

Alma frowned. "Too much to trade. I get in trouble if Pa finds out."

"This bell has a powerful conjure spell," Griff said in a coaxing voice. "It saved Wiley's life during the war. You keep it and it might help you someday too." He shook the silver bell. It made a mournful twinkle. A warm wind bent the grass. Griff shivered and put the bell back in his pocket. Everyone back home said a gust of warm air meant witches were passing. "Let's go," he said and looked about nervously. If he spied a nasty witch, he'd cross his fingers to ward off her evil eye. "Your parents are probably vexed looking for you."

Alma seemed to be considering Griff's words. At last she picked up the compass plant, took his hand, and led him down the bluff. "When do I get bell with strong medicine?"

"As soon as you give me the matches, the ax, and the cornmeal."

Alma paused to pull a spiky burr from her dress. "You like me better than Louisa?"

Griff couldn't help himself. He burst into laughter. "Why d'you ask?"

Alma pouted. "I want to know."

Griff bit his lip to keep from smiling. "I like you much better than your sister."

Alma turned and grinned slyly at him. "Then you sit by me at Grand Jubilee." Before he could answer, she raced the rest of the way down the bluff. Griff admired the wild, free way she leaped from rock to rock and waved the compass plant in the air. He jingled the bell in his pocket and followed her.

Three days before the Grand Jubilee, Elizabeth Cardwell gave birth to a baby girl. Griff and the other soldiers cheered when they heard the news. At last they had something joyous to celebrate. This would be the best Fourth of July ever. "May she prove a perfect trump!" the *Frontier Scout* declared. Toasts were given and speeches were made honoring the baby as the first white child to be born at Fort Rice.

Fourth of July dawned on a cool, uncertain morning. Thirteen guns were fired to open the festivities. The main entrance of Fort Rice was adorned with an arch of green leaves and a curved sign that said "1865" and "1776." Private Carl Muller had spent hours decorating the sign with scrolls of yellow and miniature flags. At the top of the entrance was a sign that said "Peace" with red, white, and blue stars. The sign's left pillar said "Founded," and the right pillar said "Sustained."

The troops assembled and marched around the square, then listened to Colonel Dimon's boring remarks. Griff didn't care about the blathering of the shoulder-straps. He was much more interested in the games. First prize of five Yankee dollars was offered for the person who ran fastest three times around the fort. When Griff lost, he tried the blindfolded wheelbarrow race and the sack race. Both times, he crashed into the laughing crowds. Target practice and horse racing won him one dollar in wagers. He was happy.

Mrs. Larned, Eagle Woman, Alma, and Louisa stood in the guardhouse, where they had the best view of the games. They waved handkerchiefs and cheered. Among the soldiers were frontiersmen with slouched hats, moccasins, and Canadian sashes. Friendly, trusted *waglukka* of all sizes and ages wandered about, drinking and eating and racing horses. Some had painted their faces with vermilion. Others wore a streak of red paint on the part in their hair. Most wore blankets. Lakota women and men in their finery wore fringe, beads, feathers, buffalo robes—anything that hung, shone, and fluttered. For once everyone—Indians and soldiers—seemed to be getting along.

Griff enjoyed the mock dress-parade best of all. He and the other soldiers assembled in every kind of strange outfit. Drum Major Badenhop portrayed the Colonel. He wore a yellow paper hat with a red plume, a yellow deerskin hunting shirt, white pantaloons, button-up boots, a Canadian sash with a broken sword with one foot of blade left. Private Charles Sout called himself "Sammy AAAAA General." He marched around with a cottonwood sword 15 feet long, suspenders, and a red tasseled Zouave cap. One private, claiming he was on detached service, wore a tin washbowl for a hat, and carried a crossbow to shoot rats.

Griff smeared his face and arms black as a thundercloud. He carried a broom for a gun. He wore white drawers and an old piece of overcoat on his shoulders. The other soldiers decorated themselves with war paint. They shouldered crutches, sticks, and pokers. Lucky donned a pair of buckskin breeches and tied a red comforter around his head.

Griff marched in a line as straight as a Virginia rail fence. "You fellas with the little red flags, get behind a post," Badenhop barked. "You captains, bring your guns from a left shoulder shift to a tote, and from a tote to the ground. Lay down your arms and rest."

The soldiers toppled to the ground, laughing. The comical drum corps marched down the line. "Come back, if you please," Badenhop screamed. "Attention, backsliders! Make ready to go four steps front backwards, and wait till I tells you. Make ready to git! Git! Look up towards me, and make a straight line like a tater row."

Then, as a final flourish, Sammy AAAAA General read special order 9,749,000: "Any soldier having served three years in Dacotah and re-enlisting to stay there will be considered a maniac and treated accordingly; will be shipped by first boat for the states and turned over to Barnum's Circus to act out the role of Jefferson Davis in a skeleton skit."

Everyone laughed. Everyone except Colonel Dimon, who blushed a bright red color. When he regained his composure, he ordered the assembled crowd to eat the special dinner. Alma, of course, seemed delighted to sit beside Griff. The table was heavy with slabs of buffalo and elk. As a special treat, there were expensive delicacies brought thousands of miles upriver: oyster pie; oyster stew; tapioca pudding; apple, peach, and raspberry pies; and strawberries, prunes, peaches, raisins, and figs. Griff ate until he was as full as a tick, and then he forced himself to eat some more.

The celebrating and carousing went on through the night—even after the last 13 guns were fired. Griff fell asleep atop one of the tables as the company performed a skit with Private McCarthy playing the part of Jefferson Davis, wearing boots, spurs, green goggles, a sunbonnet, a calico dress with a hoopskirt.

When Griff awoke the next day with a terrible headache, the celebrating was still continuing. He decided he needed to get himself organized. What if a steamboat arrived unexpectedly? He scooped what he could of the remaining Fourth of July feast into his knapsack, which was already packed with Wiley's map and a pistol he had "borrowed" from Captain Fay.

True to her word, Alma supplied him with the trade items she had promised in exchange for the small bell. Every day for the next four days, Griff watched the river for signs of smoke from a steamboat's smokestack and listened for the high, shrill whistle. He saw nothing.

As he was returning to the barracks feeling rather discouraged, he noticed something odd. Mrs. Larned, who was never idle for a moment, sat slumped outside her tent, her elbows on her knees, her face in her hands. She held an old flour sack to her face.

At first, Griff wondered if perhaps she had burned herself while baking. As he came closer, he heard a high-pitched lament that reminded him of his mother the day she found out his oldest brother had been killed at Bull Run.

"Mrs. Larned, ma'am?" Griff said softly. She had always been kind to him, even when he didn't have enough money for a cake. "You all right?"

Mrs. Larned rubbed her face hard with the flour sack rag, then blew her nose. Her eyes were red as if she had been crying a very long time. "Thought I'd seen all the dying I was going to for a while," she said in a hoarse voice. "Poor little babe, only seven days old."

"You don't mean the Cardwell baby, do you, ma'am?" Griff stammered.

Mrs. Larned nodded. "And her dear mother. Sweetest thing gone to rest where there's no more suffering. Just this

133

morning. I can't hardly believe it. Her husband's nearly beside himself."

Stiffly, she stood up and shoved the rag inside her apron pocket. "This country takes a heavy toll." She looked off into the distance, opened the flap to her tent, and went inside.

Griff sighed. He recalled how valiant and ridiculous Mrs. Cardwell had looked when she marched alongside her husband and the other soldiers when they made the hard trip upriver. She was such a winsome creature. Then he tried to imagine what Private Patrick Cardwell must be feeling at that very moment. Somehow, he couldn't.

The Jubilee's twined garlands of green willow hung limp and dry on the fence rails. Frayed ribbons danced and tangled in the wind. Already most of the red, white, and blue stars had blown away. Perhaps it was safer never to love at all, Griff decided, than to lose a love and feel so despondent and alone.

Chapter 13

On July 9, the same sorrowful day that Elizabeth Cardwell and her baby died, seven lodges of Blackfeet appeared on the east side of the river and set up tepees. They arrived in war jackets decorated with elk teeth, mother of pearl, beads, and porcupine quills. Around their necks hung bear-claw necklaces. Human scalp locks dangled from their spears, and eagle feathers adorned their warbonnets. Two days later, 300 more lodges appeared. Groups of Sans Arcs, Yanktonais, and Two Kettles drifted into camp. As many as 2,000 Indians were spotted along the Heart River 30 miles away, and more were drifting closer every day.

Soldiers at the fort told each other that the old warriors were arguing for peace. The young warriors wanted war. The most hostile and feared of all the tribes were the Hunkpapas, who feared a trap and refused to travel any closer than a few miles from the fort.

Soon the hills all around Fort Rice were dotted with circles of splendidly decorated tepees. Each circle opened to the east, as tradition demanded. Sioux lodges were tall and narrow with a big flap opening at the top. Cheyenne lodges were larger in circumference, shorter, with a small ventilating flap. The sky filled with smoke from cooking fires. At night, the men at Fort Rice heard the drifting sounds of dancing and drums, the plaintive singing of women, children's voices, and the barking of many dogs.

The Indians had come to meet with General Alfred Sully. Some called him "Big Heart." Sully was traveling to Fort Rice to try to strike a peace plan with the warring, starving tribes. Accompanying him were two untried companies of the 4th U.S. Volunteers.

In the barracks, no one talked about anything but Sully and the green troops that they hoped would reinforce the garrison. Sully stories abounded—how he once made mules into brevethorses, and how he was so fond of fried eggs that he carried chicken coops on every expedition. Supposedly, Sully killed two Indians and stuck their heads on spikes as a warning.

"He ain't nothing like our prim and proper colonel in dress uniform," Lucky told Griff. "Sully rigs himself out in corduroy pants stuffed in long boots, no suspenders, white shirt, and white slouch hat."

"That's right," McCarthy said, eager to tell his tale. "Once Sully met this fancy new lieutenant all dressed up in a brand-new uniform and red sash and saber belt. The fellow even went so far as to perfume himself with musk.

He goes to see Sully in his tent, and right off Sully says, 'Well, lieutenant, how long you been in the army?'

" 'Six months, sir,' says the lieutenant.

" 'Six months!' Sully roars. 'Man, I've been in the regular service twenty years and don't smell half as bad as you do!' "

Griff laughed even though he had no intention of viewing the eccentric General Sully in person. As soon as the *Belle Peoria* arrived with the detachment of new troops, he'd make his exit and escape from Fort Rice forever.

Everything seemed to be falling into place. The officers were busy organizing special feasts and peace pipe meetings on the sultry day that the *Belle Peoria* snubbed to shore. The rigging was tied, and the troops on board quickly disembarked. Up at the fort, Griff had heard that the chiefs and shoulder straps were having a big meeting. That very afternoon, Sully and his staff were going to have dinner with Colonel Dimon. The whole place was in an uproar getting ready. It would be hours before anyone would notice that Griff was missing.

He stood along the wharf, pretending to inspect the bolts of calico, barrels of salt pork, and bags of flour.

"Look lively!" a boatman shouted. "Won't be here but an hour at most. River's dropping, and we'll be lucky to reach Knife River."

"Where you headed?" Griff called, hoping he didn't sound overly interested.

"Far as we can get. Maybe Fort Union." The crew

member glanced nervously up at the tepees covering the hills. Griff knew what he was thinking. The Indians far outnumbered the soldiers. A steady stream of Indians paraded past in feathers and best dress on their way up to the fort. Some had come to hear speeches. Others came to give speeches. It was almost like the Grand Jubilee all over again, except that there was something in the air. Something Griff could not name.

"You just going to watch or do some work? Take those on board." The boatman pointed to a half-dozen large, empty wooden barrels on shore.

Griff did as he was told. He rolled each barrel up the planks, careful to shoulder his hidden knapsack on board with the last one. He looked to his right and to his left. No one in sight. He opened the barrel's lid and threw in his knapsack. Quick as a cat, he jumped inside and replaced the lid.

He crouched in the semidarkness, barely breathing for fear someone might hear him. How long? He waited for what seemed like hours. At last, the deck beneath the barrel began to rumble. The steamboat whistle sounded. Footsteps thudded past. Men shouted orders. "Dead slow!"

Finally, Griff was on his way north. He felt the pull of the current as the steamboat trembled into midstream. He leaned his head back and closed his eyes. He had not said good-bye to anyone. There was no one he would miss, he tried to convince himself. *Especially not Louisa.*

Just when he drifted into half-wakefulness, half-sleep, he heard the terrible boom of the howitzer. His head snapped forward. Instantly, the steamboat swerved then picked up speed. "Full ahead!" someone cried.

What's happening?

More voices. From faraway came the unmistakable crack of gunfire and the terrifying howling of Indian war cries. Chaos swept around him, yet Griff did not want to risk everything by poking his head out of the barrel.

"Dead slow! All hands!"

The deck shook. Griff clenched his fingers around the knapsack straps. His body was poised, ready to spring out of the barrel. *Thud!* Griff fell forward and bumped his head against the barrel wall. The boat must have hit something. He steadied himself, filled with panic that the barrel would tip and pitch him out onto the deck. The straining engine rumbled slower. Griff remembered the sound on their journey upriver. The captain was probably trying to back the boat away from a sandbar.

Gunfire smacked and ricocheted. Griff hunched down as far as his cramped space would allow. Someone was shooting at the steamboat. He knew the wooden barrel staves were no match for bullets. Carefully, he lifted the lid and peered out. Crew members dashed past with rifles and muskets. "Hunkpapas!" someone shouted.

Griff felt frozen with fear. He knew he had to get under cover, preferably behind something made of metal. As slowly as he could, he tried to untangle his sleeping legs and rise out of the barrel. From shore came another volley of shots. He leapt to the ground, dragging his knapsack with him and scuttled between another bunch of barrels toward the steamboat's center deck. He hoped he'd be safely out of range.

He sniffed. Acrid smoke filled the air. "Fire in the forward deck!" screamed a crew member. In an instant, there was splashing as men dove into the river. Others used buckets and tried to put out the flames that were quickly consuming crates of goods.

More gunfire. From where Griff hid, he couldn't tell how many Hunkpapas might be shooting at them. Was it safer to stay on board in a boat that might blow up, or risk swimming to shore and perhaps meet with the enemy head-on?

Griff crawled forward, craning his neck for a better look at the trees along the river's edge. The gunfire seemed to be coming from higher up on the bluff. If he swam to shore, maybe he'd make it safely to the trees. Somehow he'd have to try and keep his knapsack over his head to keep the hidden pistol dry. He didn't have much time. Any minute the steamboat might burst into flames, explode, and sink.

Just as he was about to lower himself into the water and head for the shore opposite the gunfire, he heard a fierce jangling. He paused and listened.

"Help!" a muffled voice cried. It seemed to be coming from one of the barrels.

Griff didn't have time to save anyone's life but his own. He lowered his feet into the Missouri, then paused. There was that strange tinny noise again. Was it a haunt?

"Help me! Oh, help me! I can't get out."

Griff pulled his feet out of the water. He scrambled closer to the barrels again. "Who are you and where you hid?"

"That you Griff?"

Griff sank back on his haunches in disbelief. Alma! He sprang to his feet and began prying lids from every barrel he could reach. Alma emerged from the last barrel. Her hair hung in limp strands around her tear-stained, dirty face. As soon as he pulled her out, she clung to him as if she might never let go.

"What you think you're doing?" he demanded angrily.

"Running away, just like you. Going to Grandmother. Not St. Louis. I—"

A bullet thudded into a barrel. Griff tackled Alma to the ground. They could hear the Indians celebrating on shore. There wasn't a moment to lose.

"Follow me," Griff said and signaled to Alma. Eagerly, she crawled beside him to the boat's edge. Already the steamboat had begun to tip precariously to one side. Bells clanged. The stern wheel paddled desperately. Griff and Alma slipped into the churning water.

She bobbed out of sight. Griff reached down to grab her. Too late.

Alma! He held the side of the boat and reached with an

outstretched arm in all directions. Nothing. When he tried to paddle farther out into the water, the heavy knapsack dragged him down. He let go of the knapsack, held his breath, and dove deep into the murky water. Desperately, he motioned his hands back and forth to try to grasp her. He knew that if the current caught her, she'd be sucked into the stern wheel's churning blades.

In the murkiness, he could see nothing, feel nothing. He came up for air and then plunged back into the water again. This time he felt something flapping limply past his hand. He held tight and pulled. She weighed practically nothing. When he burst to the surface, he gasped for breath. He held her face up with his hand under her chin. Her long hair flowed limp. She didn't move. She didn't speak. He kicked to shore allowing the current to push them down river away from the burning steamboat and the gunfire.

He stumbled into something dark and slick with plant life. A fallen tree. Gratefully, he held tight to the slimy branch with one hand and pulled himself to a standing position. With all his strength, he dragged Alma. He staggered up to the shore. Desperately, he tried to remember what happened when he was little and fell in the Pee Dee River. The brother who saved him pounded him upside down so hard that he nearly broke his rib.

With great effort Griff turned Alma upside down too. She was much heavier on land than she was in the water. He pounded her back. Brown water rushed from her mouth. She made a noise like a gasping fish. He pounded her back again.

"Stop!" she muttered. Her sandy hair was in her mouth and she could hardly talk. She crouched on the ground on her hands and knees and stared at him angrily. "Stupid *waiscus!* I'm alive!"

Griff did not know why. He began to laugh. Maybe it was the way her hair stood straight up and her dress was covered with dirt and dead leaves and twigs. Maybe it was because he had failed so miserably, and laughing was all he could do. His knapsack was gone. His pistol and his map were at the bottom of the river. His only means of escape was on fire. And now he had to return to Fort Rice with this ungrateful, foul-smelling child who blubbered and cursed him unmercifully.

Shots rang out. "Come on!" he said and grabbed Alma roughly by the arm. They scrambled into the underbrush along the shore. Mosquitoes buzzed around Griff's face. But he managed to hold very still. They could hear voices not far away. Someone was coming down the river, looking for them. Griff peeked through the leaves and saw two Indians with their faces painted red and black, floating in a bull boat down the river. They stared into the undergrowth. One paddled. The other held a rifle in readiness.

Suddenly, Griff sneezed. The sneeze was loud and uncontrollable. The Indian dipped the paddle into the water and the boat veered toward shore. Griff felt Alma's hand holding very tight to his arm. His heart beat so loudly that he was certain they would hear him. They would find them. He did not want to think what would happen then.

The Indians did not speak to one another. They drifted in silence as the round, hide-covered boat drifted closer. The boat neared shore. Swiftly, the Indian with the gun leaped to shore. He scanned the underbrush.

Alma took a handful of rocks and threw them into the moving water. *Splash! Splash!* The Indian pointed his gun. Shots rang out in quick succession into the river. Alma jumped to her feet. She shouted something to the Indian. Griff could not understand what she was saying. He stayed hunched on the ground, shivering, his hands over his head—certain that at any moment they would both be scalped.

The Indian answered Alma, and she spoke again. Her voice was loud and forceful. She kicked Griff hard and signaled for him to stand. He didn't want to. She kicked him again and he rose out of the underbrush.

The Indians came toward them. They poked Griff with the end of the rifle. Griff shivered. He raised his hands over his face as if to protect himself.

Alma shouted at the Indians again. She said something that took a very long time. The Indians put down their guns. They took a step back and looked at each other. Griff could see that they were considering her words. They spoke to one another. Then they turned to her and pointed to the boat.

To Griff's amazement, the Indians appeared to be offering them a ride. At first, he feared that they meant them harm. Were they being taken captive?

"Get in," she hissed at him. "Don't talk."

He did as she told him. It was a tight fit in the bull boat that kept moving in dizzying circles as the Indian paddled. They were going upriver now. Griff held his breath in terror. Where were they being taken?

Just below the fort a half-mile or less, the Indians brought the boat to shore. The Indian with the gun motioned for them to get out. He glanced up and down the bluffs. Quickly, Alma jumped to shore. Griff did the same. She motioned with her hand to the Indians, something that seemed almost like a farewell. Then she grabbed Griff by his arm and pulled him up toward the path to the fort.

"How did you convince them to let us go?" Griff demanded.

"I tell them my mother is The-Eagle-Woman-That-All-Look-At. They know she has strong medicine. My grandmother is Proud Walking, I tell them. My grandfather is Two Lance, chief of *Oohenonpa*. They are afraid of powerful Two Kettle tribe. They know not to harm me."

"But why didn't they kill me?" Griff asked.

Alma smiled. "I tell them you are my half-brother and have strong medicine too." She shook the little bell that still hung around her neck on a string. "You save me. I save you. Now we are even."

145

Griff grinned. Maybe he hadn't been exaggerating after all. Maybe that bell really did have a powerful conjure spell.

Chapter 14

The howitzer and the other big guns had stopped booming from the fort. But even from a distance, Griff could see that the soldiers remained in readiness. Every so often a picket could be seen passing with a gun over his shoulder. Griff pulled off his shirt, tore it in half, and tied it to a stick. This he waved in the air and shouted to the pickets, "Don't fire! Don't fire! We're friends!" He and Alma made their way inside the opened gate.

Griff felt the other soldiers' eyes staring at him and Alma as they walked through the parade grounds in their squelching and water-soaked clothing. For once he didn't care what anyone thought. He was safe. So was Alma.

Griff accompanied Alma to her family's tent. Major Galpin ran to her with open arms. He picked her up and swung her around and around.

"Mi cunk she!" her mother repeated over and over again. Her eyes filled with tears. She spoke rapidly to Alma in Lakota. Over and over, she stroked Alma's dirty face and soggy hair as if she could hardly believe that her daughter were really there.

Bashfully, Griff stepped backward. He stared at his water-logged shoes. Maybe his chance to escape was gone forever. "Griff?" someone said in a soft voice.

He looked up and saw Louisa. She held out her soft hand to shake his. He felt embarrassed. He was so dirty. For once, she didn't seem to notice. When she smiled at him, her mouth trembled slightly. "Thank you for bringing her back. You don't know how much it means to my mother and the Major. To me too."

Griff coughed self-consciously.

"She is quite precious to . . . all of us. As you can see," Louisa added quickly. She blinked hard. "Sometimes we don't know what we have until we almost lose it."

"Yes, ma'am," Griff said.

She straightened up, and the old severe expression seemed to steal across her face again. "I thought you'd like to be the first to know that I'm to be married. A captain from the 7th Iowa Cavalry. An educated man with high expectations for many promotions."

"Congratulations, ma'am," Griff replied. *Good old Louisa. Always the survivor.* "Guess you got what you always wanted."

Louisa looked at him, a bit startled.

"Just remember not to forget the ways your sister and

your mother teach you. You never know, ma'am. Someday that knowledge might save your life."

Louisa seemed so stunned, she didn't know what to say. Major Galpin rushed up to Griff and slapped him on the back. Eagle Woman cried and cried and hugged him so hard he squirmed. Griff felt light-headed as a sudden hero. He never considered himself particularly gallant. He was glad when he was able to escape back to the barracks where nobody made a fuss or asked where he'd been. Undoubtedly to McCarthy, Lucky, and the others, Griff just looked a bit dirtier than usual.

It wasn't until the next day that Griff learned what had caused the commotion at the fort the afternoon he tried to escape on the steamboat. McCarthy told him that just when General Sully and his staff crossed the river, Colonel Dimon once again displayed his remarkable talent for doing the wrong thing at the wrong time. "The fool fired a howitzer salute as soon as the ferry boat with Sully reached the landing," McCarthy said with a smirk. "The Hunkpapas, who were on their way to the fort, thought that they were being fired upon. Gave the alarm and scattered. Other Indians, who saw them running, assumed the worst and began firing from shore at the *Belle Peoria*. Luckily, the crew was able to put the fire out before it destroyed the boat and all the goods."

The rumor was that the Hunkpapas had run off and told every tribe on the Upper Missouri that General Sully had massacred all the Indians at Fort Rice.

"The good news," Lucky continued, "is that when the

peace conference ended badly, Sully got furious. Dimon may not be our officer much longer."

"I heard he's going back to the States on an important mission and a well-deserved furlough," McCarthy said and winked.

Griff had no desire to find out what would happen to Colonel Dimon. Autumn was coming. Already the nights were cool enough that it was necessary to light a fire in the barracks. He did not intend to spend another long, endless winter at Fort Rice if he could help it.

On the day the last northbound steamboat, the *Big Horn*, was due to arrive, Griff found Alma beside her family's tent. "You can't tell nobody," he whispered. On his shoulder were new supplies that he'd collected and tied inside a blanket. "I come to say goodbye. You taught me plenty about myself. I want to thank you, but I don't want you to follow me."

Alma took a deep gulp of air. She fingered the bell around her neck. "I am not going to St. Louis this year. Ma say maybe next. Louisa is teaching me to read." She looked up at him with wise dark eyes. "Griff from Carolina, you also teach me something important." She held two dirty fingers in the air. She pressed them together with her other fist. "Two parts to me. I cannot take away one without destroying the other."

Griff took a deep breath. "Never was seen the likes of you for truth-telling."

Alma seemed pleased. "I sing Brave Heart Song for you on your journey," she promised. "You are my *kola*."

"I reckon," he said and grinned.

From somewhere on the river came the haunting, urgent whistle of the *Big Horn*. Griff shifted the blanket to his other shoulder, raised one hand in farewell, and hurried down the bluff toward the Missouri.

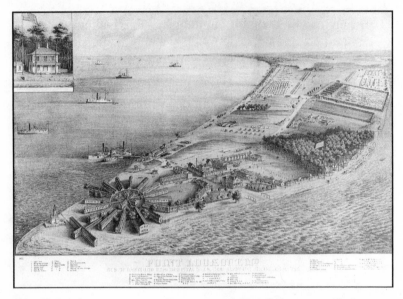

The federal prison camp for captured Confederates at Point Lookout, Maryland, in 1864. The Potomac River is to the left, Chesapeake Bay to the right. The building in the inset is the post headquarters.

This view of prison life is from a booklet of scenes painted by an unknown prisoner at Point Lookout. The numbers refer to the following captions:

1. Here's your hot coffee!

2. What's your coffee made of Mister, hard tacks or bread crust.

3. It's made of bread crust, and only one cracker a cup full.

A letter from Henry B. Dugger to his wife dated 8/06/1864
and sent while Dugger was a prisoner at Point Lookout.

Alma as a young child with her mother, Eagle Woman.

A Missouri River steamboat.

Steamboats like this supplied the Missouri River forts for more than 30 years. The spars (poles) on the foredeck were used for "grasshoppering" over sandbars. The name came from the resemblance to grasshopper legs.